M000028284

AMAZING GRACE IN THE MIDST OF GRIEF

Amazing Grace
in the Midst of Grief

JAMES L. MAYFIELD

CASCADE *Books* · Eugene, Oregon

AMAZING GRACE IN THE MIDST OF GRIEF

Copyright © 2011 by James L. Mayfield. All rights reserved. Except
for brief quotations in critical publications or reviews, no part of
this book may be reproduced in any manner without prior written
permission from the publisher. Write: Permissions, Wipf and Stock
Publishers, 199 W. 8th Ave., Suite 3, Eugene, OR 97401.

Cascade Books
A Division of Wipf and Stock Publishers
199 W. 8th Ave., Suite 3
Eugene, OR 97401
www.wipfandstock.com

ISBN 13: 978-1-60899-944-6

Cataloging-in-Publication data:

Mayfield, James L.
Amazing grace in the midst of grief / James L. Mayfield.

xxiv + 104 p.; 23 cm.

ISBN 13: 978-1-60899-944-6

Revised edition of Discovering Grace in Grief, 1994.

1. Bereavement—Religious Aspects—Christianity—Meditations.
2. Bereavement—Psychological Aspects. 3. Consolation. 4. Death—
Religious aspects—Christianity.

BF575 G7 M39 2011

Manufactured in the USA.
Scripture quotations are from the Revised Standard Version of
the Bible, copyright © 1946, 1952, and 1971 National Council of
the Churches of Christ in the United States of America. Used by
permission. All rights reserved.

This book is dedicated to my wife,
Rita Browning Mayfield,
a special gift of God's grace
to me and all who know her.

Contents

About This Book

This book has been written for those who are grieving and for those who have experienced grief. It contains more than a description of the grief process. In this book are illustrations of some ways God's grace is at work in the midst of grief—whether we are aware of it or not. In the process the truth expressed in the third verse of "Amazing Grace" is illustrated:

> Through many dangers, toils, and snares
> > I have already come;
> 'tis grace hath brought me save thus far,
> > and grace will lead me home.[1]

In order to make the book both practical and readable, I have told many stories related to various aspects of the grief process. Each of the stories is true to life in that each is rooted in actual grief experiences of one or more persons; however, each illustration or story has been modified (except for those about my experiences) and all the names have been changed in order to protect identities and privacy.

1. John Newton, "Amazing Grace," in *The United Methodist Hymnal* (Nashville: United Methodist Publishing House, 1989), 378.

A version of this book was first published in 1994 by Upper Room Press with the title *Discovering Grace in Grief.* That version has gone out of print. When it was no longer available through Upper Room Press, I began to receive requests for copies from churches that had used it as part of their ministry to families in grief and from individuals who had found the book helpful and wanted to give a copy to a friend or family member going through grief.

The frequency of these requests motivated me to explore the possibility of republishing the book. However, as I reread what I had written years ago, I discovered I was no longer satisfied with the way I had expressed some of my thoughts in the original manuscript, and that the book would be improved by the rearrangement of some chapters. Also I have learned more about both grief and grace through my personal experiences and through the experiences of others I served as pastor. In addition, I became aware of certain deficiencies in the earlier version. This volume contains these revisions and additions.

I am grateful to all the people who have allowed me to be their pastor as they made their journey through grief, especially members of St. Andrew's United Methodist Church in San Antonio, Texas; First United Methodist Church in Mathis, Texas; First United Methodist Church in Port Lavaca, Texas; Northwest Hills United Methodist Church in Austin, Texas; and Tarrytown United Methodist Church in Austin, Texas. Through their experiences of grief and God's grace in the midst of grief, I learned much. I am also grateful to Captain Larry Greenslit, US Navy chaplain, for sharing some experiences of his dealing with the grief of spouses and of families of Marines killed in military action.

—Jim Mayfield

Introducing Grief and Grace

Grief Is More Than Sadness

Although it is not unusual for us to mean "sorrow" or "sad" when we speak of "grief" or "grieving," the truth is sorrow is only one part of a complex process. Grief involves much more than sorrow or sadness.

Grief Is a Time of Transition

From my experiences in grief I have come to view grief as a special time of transition. For example, when my Dad died, my relationship with him did not end; it changed. It changed from a relationship with someone I could see with my eyes, touch with my hands and hear with my ears to a relationship with a *living memory*. I call it a "living memory" because my memory of Dad is not limited to remembering past experiences, such as our going fishing when I was a child. It is a living memory in that it not only provides me with wisdom and wit from the past but also engages me where I am in the present. In my mind's eye, I envision the smile on his face and the delight in his eyes as he responds to his great granddaughters, born three decades after his death. The memory of him is so alive in me, I can almost hear him speaking to me as I deal with whatever I must face.

The process of grief I experienced in the months following his death was a process in which my relationship with this man I could physically touch became a relationship with a memory that remains very much alive in me.

A significant relationship does not end when someone we love dies as much as it changes from a relationship with a person of flesh and blood to a relationship with a living memory. Life goes on and our relationship with that person goes on.

Sometimes the Memories Are Painful

I am aware there are those whose relationship with their fathers (or whoever) was painful. For example, I remember a friend who was abused as a child by her father when he was drunk, and he was all too often drunk. She both hated and loved her father. His death did not magically undo the damage that had been done by him when she was a child. Her love-hate relationship with her father continued to influence her responses to others—especially men. She discovered that even though he was dead, she still needed to work through her relationship with him. She became active in the Al-Anon program for adult children of alcoholics and with additional help from counseling, she reached a point of genuine forgiveness that set her free from bondage to the painful experiences that had influenced so much of her living. Although her father was dead, her relationship with him changed. In her reaching a point of forgiveness, she was not only set free from bondage to resentments but was also able to draw wisdom from her memories.

I have also known individuals who had painful memories but did not work through them and remained in bondage to them. Although the one who had hurt them was dead, the memory of the hurt they had received was very much alive and influenced the way they responded to life.

A significant relationship does not end when the other person in that relationship dies. What happens is that the relationship changes from a relationship with a person to a relationship with a living memory. Life goes on, and through our living memory of that person our relationship with that person goes on.

Grief Is Complex

Grief is complex and can be chaotic. In this book that identifies various aspects of the grief experience and ways God's grace can be at work in our grief, one might be tempted to assume the various experiences in grief come one after another in the order presented in this book. However the experience of grief is not like a stairway in which one first takes "this step," then "that step" and then "the next," until one has completed the stages like climbing stairs.

As all who have gone through grief know, grieving is not that orderly and neat. Grief is a long, complex experience, and the more intense the grief, the longer it takes. The best metaphor I have for describing the grief process is a complex tangle of different-colored threads, strings and yarn. In each tangle, one can see each of the different-colored strands, but one cannot pull a single strand out of the tangle and isolate it. To deal with one thread, one has to deal with the whole tangle.

Not only is our experience of grief complex; each time we go through grief we have a different experience. No two people responding to the same loss will experience grief the same way, and each time we experience grief we experience a different tangle. No one can predict how grief will be experienced by himself or herself, much less by someone else. This time red is a tiny thread and not as obvious as some of the other colors, but the next time the red strand may be a thick woolen yarn that is highly visible.

Strands in the Tangle of Grief

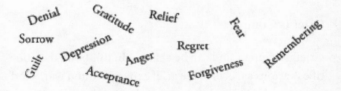

The Greater the Grief, the Longer the Process

There is no set timetable for the complex process of grief. However, the greater one's sense of loss is, the longer that experience of the grief process is likely to be. Part of what this means in our society for those in grief is that within a relatively short period of time most of their friends and neighbors will be insensitive to what they are going through. It is not that the friends and neighbors do not care as much as it is that they are focused on their own lives and they simply forget and/or they are unaware of how long and complex the process of grief is.

It has not always been that way in our society. In pre-World War II in rural central Texas it was assumed and expected that when a spouse died the surviving spouse would wear black in social gatherings for twelve months. I remember overhearing some of my grandmother's friends talking in shocked tones about a woman who had come to worship wearing a brightly colored dress although it had been less than a year since her husband's funeral.

There was folk-wisdom at work in that custom of expecting surviving spouses to wear black for twelve months. People knew grieving took time. Wearing black for twelve months in social settings was a cue to help the friends and neighbors remember the person in black was still going through the long process of grief.

I do not want to revive the rigid social custom of the surviving spouse being expected (unofficially required) to wear only black in social settings for twelve months. Yet, our abandoning that custom did have its price. Today, within a relatively short period of time, friends and neighbors tend to be insensitive to the grieving that is still taking place.

Varieties of Causes for Grief

Grief is a powerful and complex experience that happens to us when we have suffered a significant loss. Some form of death has happened, but it is not only the death of a person that can send us into grief. It can be the loss of a job, the loss of a dream, the end to a friendship, the loss of youth, or the loss or "death" of something else. Whenever we experience the loss of something or someone important to us, we experience grief. And although the primal cause of grief is the death of someone we love, the experience of grief can also be triggered by other significant losses.

Some Examples

Louise did not have many close friends in the small town where she lived. She loved books, ideas, and art. Most of the women in her community had never developed these interests. There was one exception: Margaret. She was the one person in the town with whom Louise felt close. Then, Margaret's husband changed jobs, and they moved far away. Louise experienced loss and the anguish of grief.

Bill and Mary were divorced. Although Bill was convinced the divorce was the best solution for everyone concerned, he grieved over the failure of the marriage. He grieved over the death of a dream.

It was the pocketknife that my grandfather had used as a rancher. I had been very close to my grandfather. The knife was one of the last gifts he gave me. I kept it in my desk drawer and used it to open boxes and letters. One day the knife was gone. It was only a knife, but it had special significance to me. I grieved when I lost it.

When I was in high school, the girl I was dating told me that she did not want to "go steady" with me anymore. For days I experienced a terrible ache. Some call that experience "a broken heart." Today I realize I was experiencing grief.

Anytime a significant loss causes us to experience deep sorrow or anguish or remorse, we are in grief. It may be a financial loss, a job loss, the loss of health, the loss of some desired possibilities, the loss of hope, or the loss of a friendship. Grief can be caused by retirement or divorce or business failure or . . . (fill in the blank). Any loss that is a significant loss to us personally can trigger the grief experience.

Grief Can Be Destructive

Mrs. Martin was very close to her husband. They had been friends, lovers, husband and wife, for more than forty years. When Mr. Martin died, Mrs. Martin went into the dark valley of grief and stayed there. Years later, she was still there. For the remainder of her life she refused to mix with other people. She kept the shades pulled down in her house. Her conversations focused on the events of years ago. Like singing the refrain of a song, she said over and over: "I don't know what I'll do without him."

Mr. Lucas is a bitter man. He hates the large company that has employed him the last twenty-five years. He feels the company has ruined his life. Years ago, when Mr. Lucas graduated from college with highest honors, he went to work for this large company and expected quickly to become a top executive. Other people thought the same thing. But something happened. After a few promotions a position Mr. Lucas really wanted was given to the son of one of the company's vice presidents. Mr. Lucas went into grief, and his grief was most frequently experienced in feelings of anger and resentment. Mr. Lucas never fully recovered. In his grief (seen by others as bitterness), he began to withdraw. He felt his dreams crumbling. His humor began to have a cutting, angry edge to it. He was "passed over" again. His bitterness increased. He was "passed over" again and again.

Grief can be a destructive force—something that tears people apart, tears down life, and sets in motion responses that make life worse. Grief can rob life of its potential. It can twist healthy personalities into sick distortions.

But grief can also be a time in which we grow in wisdom and grace. The painful experience of grief can be suffering that ultimately deepens our faith, expands our capacity to receive God's grace, and brings out the best within us.

Grief Does Not Have to Be Destructive

Although grief can be destructive, it does not have to be. *God does not abandon us to the destructive power in grief.* Throughout the Bible many passages remind us that God's grace is with us. One of the most familiar verses is found in the Twenty-Third Psalm:

> Even though I walk through the valley of the shadow
> of death,
> I will fear no evil [destruction];
> for thou art with me;
> thy rod and thy staff,
> they comfort me. (RSV)

This has been a very meaningful Scripture verse for me. It helped me deal with my grief when Dad died. In helping me come to terms with that grief, it helped me come to terms with some of the other experiences of grief in my life.

In this familiar verse, the poet not only declares God will be with us in that dark valley, he also gives us some clues about how God will be there. God will be there like a shepherd with a rod and a staff. God will be there with the tools needed to fight off the wolves (a rod) and with the tools needed to push us on when we are ready to quit or to pull us through the tight places in life (a staff).

The tools I see God using are people. Some people have been the instruments God has used in my life like the shepherd's rod and staff. At times they have been used by God like the shepherd's rod: to defend me from the "wolves" I did not have sense enough to avoid. At other times they have been like the shepherd's staff God used to push me on when I was ready to give up, or to pull me through the narrow squeezes in my life. God has worked through persons to protect me and move me through the valley.

"Thy rod and thy staff, they comfort me." Comfort is not the same thing as sympathy. A sympathetic person may cry because I am crying; however, a person who comforts me is a person who gives me the strength to face what must be faced and the power to move on. When I am comforted, I discover I have what is needed to face life as it really is, and that I have what I need in order to move on in search of constructive possibilities. When we are comforted, we are strengthened to face reality and empowered to move ahead.

When Dad died I needed comforting. I needed strength to face reality and power to move on. The year before we discovered he had lung cancer, our relationship had moved to a new level. No longer were we merely father and son but also one adult enjoying relationship with another adult. We appreciated each other's knowledge and abilities. Just as we were beginning to enjoy this new dimension of our relationship, he died. My grief was severe.

Then the people came with their hugs and fumbled words. They sent cards and brought cakes and made awkward visits. Here and there in the midst of all these gestures of sympathy and love, I was comforted. Exactly how it happened is a mystery to me. Two persons could do the same thing, and through the actions of one I would receive only sympathy, but through the actions of the other I would be comforted.

In the Gospel of John, a word Jesus used to describe the Holy Spirit can be translated as "the comforter"—the one who strengthens and empowers (John 14:26). How the Spirit is at work in our lives is a mystery, beyond our control. Jesus told Nicodemus the work of the Spirit is like the wind; no one can say where it is coming from or where it is going (John 3:8). In my grief I could not say when or from whom my comfort would come. But it came—more often than not as a surprise.

To say the comfort I received was merely the by-product of the words and deeds of friends and family is inadequate and therefore inaccurate. It was something more than their words and deeds that comforted me. I understand this "something more" to be the grace of God that was at work in the midst of their words and deeds.

It was the grace of God, the work of the Holy Spirit. Through their love, God's love was given and I discovered—bit by bit—that I could face my loss and move on. I was comforted.

An Audacious Claim

It is audacious of me to claim God has been active in my life, in our lives. Such audacity is not the conclusion of rational argument as much as it is the by-product of faith, a by-product of confidently trusting God and God's grace. Through my experience of grief, I gained a new sense of what it means to speak of God at work among us and through us. I am convinced the comfort (strength and empowerment) I received through the words and deeds of my friends was an expression of the grace of God at work in and through their love.

The grace of God I experienced in my grief other persons have experienced in theirs. It is these experiences that have led me to believe that God's grace can be discovered in *all* grief. Nothing separates us from the love of God (Romans 8:38–39)—not even our grief.

What Is God's Grace?

In my search to find the best way to describe or define grace I looked in several books. The most helpful definition I found was in *The Interpreter's Dictionary of the Bible:*[1]

1. The following list is paraphrased from C. L. Mitton, "Grace," in

(1) Grace is a free gift and unearned.

(2) Grace is an abundant gift, a gift far larger than we can ever imagine.

(3) Grace is received through faith.

(4) Grace is an active and effective power from God, bringing merciful aid to persons.

The fourth statement about grace is the one that is emphasized in this book. *Grace* is the word I use to point toward the mysterious healing, redeeming, reconciling, empowering activity of God at work in our lives.

Who can count the ways God reaches out toward us, offering wholeness to our brokenness, fulfillment to our emptiness, purpose to our sense of futility? *Grace* is the word I use to point toward the mysterious healing, redeeming, reconciling realities at work in our lives. This grace expresses itself in the words and actions of people but it is more than their words and deeds. God's grace is in the various realities symbolized and expressed in giving a cup of water to the thirsty. This grace also reveals itself in the cluster of meanings we can discover in the sacraments. This grace is revealed in stories and insights from the Scriptures. This grace is both celebrated and discovered in various acts of worship. Through the struggles and the calms in a life of prayer, grace comes.

It is no easier to say what grace is than it is to say what a mother's love is. A mother's love is never seen; only the fruits or by-products of her love are visible. We see her taking care of her children: feeding them, nursing them

---

The Interpreter's Dictionary of the Bible, ed. George Arthur Buttrick (New York: Abingdon, 1962), 2:466.

when they are sick, worrying and searching for them when they are lost, scolding and disciplining them when they are misusing their lives. We see only signs of love and the signs alone are not her love. Her love is more than any expression of it. Her love is invisible. It is beyond measuring, beyond the categories of proof.

God's grace is the activity of God's love. We do not deserve it; we cannot earn it. It is there and here, then and now. Like a mother's love, all we can see are by-products; all we can see are signs. Only through the eyes of faith can the significance of the signs be discovered.

In this little book I am making no effort to prove God's grace is active in our lives. This is assumed. What I will do is describe a few situations that may happen as we experience grief and say: "Hey, isn't this one of the fruits of grace? Isn't this another sign of God's love, God's grace, at work in our lives?"

1   *Entering Grief*

"I Can't Believe It"

When we experience significant loss suddenly and unexpectedly, we often have difficulty grasping the reality of
what has happened. Our denial is not refusing to believe as
much as it is an inability to believe.

"I was numb. I couldn't believe it. I heard the doctor.
My mind comprehended what he was telling me but I felt
as if I were an outside observer. It seemed that all this was
happening to someone else.

"I heard him ask me if I was all right and I heard myself say: 'I'm okay; I'll make it.' I could see clearly. I could
hear and yet I felt as if I were in some kind of a fog. Some
of the neighbors were with me. Most of them were crying.
I wondered what was wrong with me because I was not
crying. After all, Nancy was my wife.

"It seemed an eternity ago that the phone call brought
me to the hospital. I looked at my watch; it had only been a
couple of hours. 'Nothing we can do,' the doctor had said.
'Massive head injuries.'

"All this cannot be happening, but it is. I must make myself think. What do I need to do? Nancy wanted to go out Friday. We won't be doing that. I've got to think of other things. What shall I tell the kids? What am I going to do with the children while I am at work? I wonder if we have enough milk at home for their breakfast tomorrow. Nancy took care of things like that.

"I hear myself responding to some friends: 'I just can't realize it. I know it has happened. It just does not seem real.'"

Our initial reaction to an unexpected death is usually one of shock and numbness. We hear ourselves saying: "I just can't believe it happened."

Denial beyond the Initial Phase of Grief

Our experience of denial is not limited to our initial response to the death of someone we love. It can also be experienced much later in the grief process. For example, my mother died in January, but nine months later I experienced denial. It was a Saturday afternoon; I was taking a shower after having spent much of the day working in the yard; the thought came in my mind: "When I get dressed, I ought to call Mother." Often on Saturday afternoons Rita and I had talked with her on the phone. Of course, almost as soon as I had the idea of calling her, I remembered she had died nine months earlier. There was still a part of me that was resisting the reality of her having died. We want to hang on to what we love. Even today, many years later there are moments when I find it hard to believe she is dead.

"I Am So Relieved"

Another initial response to the death of someone we love can be relief, especially if the process of dying was prolonged and involved suffering.

"Thank God it's over." The thought played in her mind like a stuck record. How long had it been? Mrs. Wallace had lost track of the days, the weeks, the months. For a while her father would be in a nursing home, and then he would be back in the hospital. The cycle was repeated again and again. It seemed like a long, slow, endless treadmill between the hospital and the nursing home.

Mrs. Wallace had watched her father change from a strong, independent person into a weak and helpless infant. She saw him change from a person who enjoyed life and people into a person who was suspicious and afraid. Although she had responsibilities for her children and a part-time job, Mrs. Wallace visited him at least once a day, usually twice. But he became forgetful, and he would forget her having been to see him. Several times he was angry with her and accused her of not caring. He even *believed* she did not care. In tears he told her that he wished he could die and not be a bother to her any more.

Little by little, he lost touch with reality. At first it was present reality that he lost. His mind returned to his past. He relived events and conversations that had taken place many years ago. Toward the end, he even lost touch with the past. He lay in bed and stared blankly into space. It was painful to Mrs. Wallace to watch her father's mind and body deteriorate. The process of his dying was so slow. Finally death came.

Exhausted physically and emotionally, Mrs. Wallace felt as if a huge weight had been lifted from her shoulders. She felt so relieved that she worried about herself: "What is wrong with me? I loved Dad. Shouldn't I feel more sadness? All I feel is relief. If I feel anything it is more of a feeling of gladness. I'm glad my ordeal is over. I'm glad his ordeal has come to an end. Is that wrong?"

Gifts and Problems

Our initial responses to a significant loss can be viewed as gifts. When death is a sudden, unexpected event, our numbness can be seen as a gift of calmness that will allow us to absorb what has happened; it even allows us to take care of some practical questions before we are hit by the emotional storms. When the death has been anticipated for some time, the relief we may experience can be understood as the gift of a brief rest between the ordeal of anticipating a significant loss and the ordeal of adjusting to the implications that loss has for our living. Thus, our initial experience of grief can be seen as a gift of God's grace.

However, we sometimes have problems in this first part of our grief experience. Sometimes the problems stem from misunderstanding our feelings and our reactions to what people around us say and do.

If we view our initial reaction to death and loss as our primary and fundamental response, we may be in for some problems. Taken out of the context of the total grief experience, our initial reactions may cause us to enter grief with a low opinion of ourselves.

For example, if we think our initial numbness is our primary response to the loss rather than merely the way this experience of grief is beginning, we may view ourselves as being insensitive and begin to wonder if we are selfish, unloving persons. When we confuse the way our grief begins for the total grief experience, we are likely to add the burden of low self-esteem to the burden of our grief.

Our initial reaction to death is precisely that—our *initial* reaction. To view it as the primary or fundamental expression of our deepest self is to misunderstand what is happening, and it is to be vulnerable to additional problems.

In this situation we may also misunderstand other people's attempts to help us. In their desire to be helpful and supportive they will sometimes view the exterior behavior of our initial response and make comments such as: "You are so strong!" or "I certainly admire the way you are taking this." or "For you to be so calm, your faith must be very deep."

If we are already feeling some form of mild guilt because we misunderstand our numbness or relief, these well-intentioned compliments may pour more fuel on the fire of our feelings of guilt. They tell us we are strong and that we have faith, but we see ourselves as being insensitive and selfish. In this situation the compliments make us feel guilty because of the gap between their description of us and our image of ourselves. If we listen only to the words our friends say, their comments are likely to be misunderstood. If that happens, their gestures of friendship will be significantly less helpful than they were intended to be.

"You are so strong!" may say to us, "Hold all your emotion in; do not let it splash on other people."

"I certainly admire the way you are taking this," may say to us: "I accept your grief so long as it does not bother me. Keep it to yourself."

"Your faith is so strong!" may say to us: "It is your Christian duty to be a silent, smiling rock. Faith does not know sorrow."

When we listen only to the *words* of our friends, we are setting ourselves up for misunderstanding because in our focusing only on their words, we tend to be insensitive to the concern and love behind their words. When this happens, we are likely to miss the most important message our friends are attempting to share.

When we misunderstand the comments (as illustrated above), we are likely to be caught somewhere between not liking ourselves because we are not living up to what we think is their image of us, and trying to pretend to be the person we think they want us to be. The result of these misunderstandings is a loss of intimacy that tends to make us feel isolated rather than comforted. Later, during the emotional storms of sorrow and anguish when we need to reach out to others, we may feel cut off.

To prevent this from happening, we need to see our initial reaction to loss as only the first phase of grief, and when others say whatever they say, it is most helpful for us to focus primarily on their intention to express friendship and love. Our friends who love us are not trying to set us up as ideal super-humans. They are not trying to cut us off. They are reaching out in compassion to give us support. We need to be sensitive to their intentions. It is the reality

of their love—more than their particular words or deeds—
that gives us what we need in our grief.

Grace and Faith

When we are touched by the love of our friends, we are
also touched by the grace of God. All this love we receive
by faith. We *trust* we are loved; it is a leap of faith. We *trust*
that somewhere within the poorly chosen words and awkward acts there is the gift of love our friends are offering to
us. We have no illusions that the love we receive from our
friends is totally free from their self-interest, but (hope-
fully) we are also free from the cynicism that focuses only
on the imperfection and self-interest that may be there.
Human love is seldom perfect, but that does not negate
the love that is there. Within the faults, failures, and sins
of our imperfect friends and family members are also their
genuine expressions of compassion and love. By faith we
receive the love reflected in their words and deeds.

When we are touched by the love of our friends, we
are also touched by the grace of God and through that love
we are empowered us to face what has to be faced, and
move on. How the grace of God is at work through family
and friends is a primary and even primal mystery. It cannot be proven to the skeptic (a fact that is frustrating to
both the skeptic and the faithful). Just as a mother's love
cannot be finally proven and just as the love of a friend
can be perceived only through faith, so also the grace of
God cannot be proven to someone who is committed to
the belief that God's love is only a sentimental illusion. Yet
God's grace is as real as the love within a healthy family

and among true friends, providing what we need in the midst of our grief. It takes only the eyes of faith to recognize the deeper dynamic that is happening.

Summary

Through the initial experiences of grief God's grace is at work among us. God's grace is in the gift of numbness or relief. God's grace is in our friends' responses. Even when their love is inadequately expressed, God can use it to give us the grace we need. All this grace we receive by faith. We trust we are loved; we trust we can love, and through this faith, we move on.

2 *Dealing with Memories*

A Lot of Remembering

When Dad died, our family gathered, and friends came by. We were drawn together by the power love has when it becomes grief. Each of us had been touched by Dad's living. Now he was dead, and we would miss him. The closer we were to him, the greater our pain.

United in our grief, we felt close to one another. The distinction between friends and family seemed to melt. Affection and sympathy urged us to touch each other. When we shook hands there was an added touch. More often than usual we would embrace and kiss. Sometimes this was done in silence, our tears speaking for us. Sometimes someone said: "I'm sorry." or "Is there anything we can do?" or simply "Oh, Jim."

Once we passed the initial greeting, we expressed the love that brought us together by talking about Dad. It was not a planned or calculated ritual. It was the natural thing to do. Without realizing how we started, my mother or one of my sisters or I would discover ourselves retelling the story of Dad's dying. We seemed compelled to tell it, and those who had come seemed eager—not just eager, needing—to hear it.

Over and over we told the story of the medical examination, the grim report, our difficulty believing the bad news, the efforts to find a cure, the bravery of Dad, the ordeals in the hospital, and finally the story about the night he died.

After some comments or questions, the conversation usually drifted toward some pleasant memories: "Remember the time he took us fishing?" Or, "Remember how he loved watermelon? Well, one time . . ." or "Did I ever tell you about the time he . . . ?"

We shared our memories. Many of them caused us to smile or laugh. Sometimes the memories woke such feelings of affection or pride that tears came and it was difficult to talk. In all this it was as if we had an inner compulsion to remind ourselves about who Dad was, and what he meant to our lives. At other times it seemed we used our conversations as a way to allow the reality of his death to soak in.

As we move through the process of grief, we do a lot of remembering. Why? I think our "remembering when" is a vital part the transition from our relationship with someone we can see and touch to our relationship with a living memory. (See "Introducing Grief and Grace.")

Several factors stimulate our memories. Because of the death, daily routine is interrupted, and our attention is focused on one specific relationship. The spotlight of our emotions is on our memories of past experiences with that person. Even after the funeral when we return to our routine responsibilities, much of the time our emotional focus center on what we have lost. While we are going through grief, whenever the demands of our daily responsibilities let up, we frequently find ourselves involved in "remembering when . . ."

Other people stimulate our memories. Death often puts us in contact with persons from our past. Family members and friends we have not seen or heard from in a long time visit or send us an e-mail or call. These people from our past wake our sleeping memories. Experiences and events we have not thought about in years flood into our minds. Remembering is stimulated even more by our conversations. As one story is told, it triggers the memory of another. We talk about the past experiences we share. At times the stories reveal insights we did not know about the one who died.

When the Memories Are Pleasant

Our telling stories is not merely an activity of remembering; it is a way of celebrating—a by-product of our love for the one who died and a reflection of our gratitude. Sometimes our stories reflect the special pride we feel about the way this person we loved lived and some of what he or she accomplished in life. It is not unusual in our "remembering when" for us to discover or rediscover wisdom for living.

Not All Memories Are Pleasant

Not all our memories are pleasant. Dad died in my arms, struggling for breath. That experience was not a pleasant one. As I moved beyond the first days of grief, I remembered ways I had let Dad down. I remembered childhood lies I told. I remembered his anger toward me when he blamed me for breaking a tool I had not broken or even used. I remembered from childhood how I resented Dad not taking time to play with me the way the next-door father did with his sons. Dad always seemed too busy. Not all memories are pleasant.

There may be some remembering we do at a level below or beyond our consciousness. For several weeks after Dad died, I had nightmares. I would suddenly wake, knowing I had a terrible dream but unable to recall what it was. I was thirty-one when he died. Only within his last year had we begun to experience an adult-to-adult relationship. We both realized I was beyond adolescence. There was respect as well as affection in our relationship. I think I did not want to remember some of the past tension and problems, and yet I needed to work through them. So, my guess is that I was doing that through dreams. As I moved on through my grief, the dreams no longer disturbed my sleep.

Bill's father had been both emotionally and physically abusive—especially when he was drunk. When his father died, Bill was an adult. As an adult he was still struggling with his longing to love his father and to be loved by him. Bill was also struggling with his anger and resentment rooted in memories of physical and emotional pain his father had caused. The two men seldom saw each other once Bill left home. If his father had any feelings of regret or remorse, he never shared them with Bill. (See chapters 6 and 7 below.)

When his father died, Bill's memories were so filled with the residue of past pain that when others would say something nice about his father, it triggered feelings of anger and bitterness. Rather than feeling comfort, Bill wanted to say: "Oh, if you only knew the truth about him." When others offered him sympathy and affection, Bill's response was distant. It was as if he was afraid to trust the compassion of anyone.

Sometimes the memories of what was done or not done in the past can tempt us to become bitter and crippled by those memories; we find it difficult to risk trusting others and hampered in our ability to receive and give love.

Because unpleasant memories can be so very painful, we are tempted to deny them. One of the dangers in denying our painful memories is that if we fail to deal with the pain in our past, the pain in our past will influence our living without us being aware of it. The painful experiences in Bill's past did not evaporate simply because he suppressed his memory of them. They influenced his attitude and outlook on life and thus impacted his interaction with others.

Sometimes the painful memories are related more to what we have done or failed to do than to the behavior of the one who died. Mary remembers the ugly words she said to her father. It was difficult for them to visit without having a disagreement that deteriorated into angry confrontations in which hurtful words were exchanged. If they had a peaceful visit, it was because both of them avoided all the sensitive topics, or because they were less than candid with one another.

Mary remembers the hurt she caused her father. She remembers the pain her behavior caused him, and her angry explosion of words when he expressed his disapproval. She remembers how their relationship was, and she blames herself. The ache in her grief reinforced her low opinion of herself. Her regret over what she did as well as what she failed to do placed on her a heavy load of guilt. When she dreamed about the relationship that might have been (perhaps could have been), her regret evolved into self-contempt.

Not all her unpleasant memories were "her fault." Some of the unpleasant memories were of her father hurting her. For example, in his anger he had told her he did not think she would ever amount to much as a teacher. He accused her of being insensitive, impractical, and hotheaded. "All you can do is hurt people," he said. Mary remembers, and the pain in her grief is increased by the burden of self-doubt and guilt. "Maybe he was right."

Unpleasant memories can be a negative force. When the source of our unpleasant memories is ourselves, we remember our bad decisions and the hurt we caused, or the good we failed to do. We can be haunted by the words we failed to say and condemned by our guilt. When the source of our unpleasant memories is the one who died, we remember the disappointment, heartache and pain he/she caused and are tempted to bog down in resentment, bitterness and unresolved anger.

Potential Problems in "Good Memories"

However, good memories can also cause problems. Our pleasant memories can shackle us to the past. In chapter 1 the experience of Mrs. Martin was described. When her husband died, she lost herself in good memories, which over time became idealized; her memories idealized their past and reflected the way she wished life had been as much as or more than the way it had been. Mrs. Martin lived the rest of her life in such bondage to her good memories and her idealized memories that she was unable to move on with her life and embrace new possibilities and opportunities.

The more she focused on how good the old days were with him, the more she came to believe she could not face new days without him. The more she focused on how much he had done for her and how she had depended on him, the more she doubted that she could make it by herself. Her pleasant memories created the illusion of a safe, secure, and happy past she did not want to leave. So rather than moving on with her life, nourished by her good memories, she allowed herself to be imprisoned by those memories and unable to embrace new possibilities.

Pleasant memories sometimes tempt us to so idealize the past that we are paralyzed and unable to deal with present realities or to see the opportunities we are being given.

Memories and Grace

Remembering is a gift of grace, a good gift; but like all gifts it can be misused. But it does not have to be a negative force. Remembering can be one of the tools God uses to enable us to deal with our loss in a positive way.

It is easy to see how grace comes through our pleasant memories. From them we discover some of the good gifts that have come into our lives for which we can be thankful. As we remember the good times, we often rediscover experiences in life that make living a joy. Such memories can lead to insights that influence us to rearrange our priorities. As we see good aspects of our relationship with the one who died, we become more aware of the great potential in all our relationships. The awareness of this potential can excite us to improve our relations with others.

When people talked about Tom's father, all the memories seemed to illustrate how hard he tried to be fair and just in all situations. This was a characteristic that Tom admired. Remembering the example set by his father, Tom rededicated himself to be that kind of an example for his son.

Even our unpleasant memories can be a means of grace. As we remember the imperfections in our relationship, we can obtain wisdom. Our unpleasant memories can motivate us to change patterns in our behavior. Unpleasant memories can be God's gift that causes us to decide to change, to become better people. They can be the catalyst that moves us toward forgiving what needs forgiveness so that we are set free from old angers and resentments and empowered to move on in our living.

When grief brings to the surface painful memories of what the one who died had done, we are being offered an opportunity to deal with those memories. Basically we have two choices: to forgive whatever needs to be forgiven, or to hang on to anger and resentment.

It is God's grace at work in life (and in grief) that can empower us to let go of our painful past—to forgive whoever needs forgiving (others or ourselves or both). Forgiveness does not change the past, nor does it free us from consequences of past wrongs.

For example, Bill's father lost the homestead; Bill's forgiving him does not undo the loss. Nor does Bill's forgiveness change his father. What Bill's forgiveness does is set Bill free from bondage to the hurt he received from his father. By forgiving his father, Bill is set free from his bondage to bitterness and resentment. In his freedom from resentments, Bill is able to draw on the wisdom to be gained from his painful memories.

God's grace can be at work in the midst of our remembering. It is grace working through our painful memories that enables us to move on with greater wisdom. It is grace working through our good memories that leads us to a greater sense of appreciation, gratitude, and sometimes inspiration.

Grace through Shared Memories

God's grace is present in the love we receive from family and friends. As our friends and family share their memories with us and we share ours with them, we are united in a common experience. Through this mutual sharing, our loneliness is overcome and we are helped to feel less vulnerable.

As we tell each other our memories, we can discover new insights into the one who died and even insights about ourselves. As we experience the special fellowship of grief, we can experience a depth of compassion that brings us a sense of peace. God's grace is at work in this sharing that gives us peace and strength. God's grace is at work in whatever enables us to realize we are not totally alone.

The Significance of Seeking

What is the factor that makes our "remembering when" a positive force? What keeps our remembering from being a negative influence in our living? The answer to this mystery includes something about our expectations. Discovering grace in our memories is related to whether or not we are looking for it.

Jesus talked about the importance of what we are looking for. He said: "Blessed are those who hunger and thirst for righteousness, for they shall be satisfied" (Matthew 5:6). We who long for, who look for (who hunger and thirst for) a good relationship with God (righteousness) are going to be satisfied. That is the promise in this beatitude. "Seek and you will find," Jesus said (Matthew 7:7).

Discovering grace in our "remembering when" is related to what we are looking for in our memories. If we are not looking for a pearl, we are likely to swallow it with the oyster. If we are looking for the grace of God, we are much more likely to recognize it at work in our lives. After all, the grace of God is at work in all things—even our "remembering when."

3 *Weathering the Emotional Storm*

There is an emotional storm within the grief process, and it breaks loose when the extent of what we have lost becomes an emotional reality within us. As we become aware of how much we miss the one who died, and how much more we will miss that person in the future, waves of sorrow overwhelm us like the waves of a hurricane overwhelm whatever is in its path. Sometimes the storm is made more intense by our awareness of potential that was left unfulfilled. This is especially true when the one who died was young. Sometimes the storm of sorrow is made more intense as we realize our dreams related to that person will never be fulfilled. My mother's sorrow was made more intense as she realized Dad's death meant the dreams she and he had worked toward would never be fulfilled.

As the news of the death of someone we dearly love moves from being information in our heads to being a reality we feel in the pit of our stomach, we experience the emotional storm of sorrow. The storm rages inside us. There is hurt, ache, emptiness, turmoil deep within us.

Delayed Storms

Sometimes this storm is delayed in coming. This was my experience related to my mother's death. During the last two years of her life, she suffered increasing dementia. From time to time she would ask me to do something for her. A few days later when I reported what had been done, she would become angry, accusing me of taking over and making decisions that were hers to make. I began to take my wife or one of my sisters as a witness so that later when she did not remember having made the decision, I would have some support in convincing her that I had merely done what she had asked. However, when I did this, the result was that she became depressed. "I'm just losing my mind, and you all would be better off with me dead," she would say through tears. I did not know which was worse to deal with—her anger or her depression.

Daily my mother prayed that she would die before totally losing her mind, and that she would not die alone. Both prayers were given an affirmative answer.

The evening she died we had been having a happy visit, remembering old times and laughing about antics of children and grandchildren. All of a sudden she burped and out came some blood. More came and within seconds she was unconscious. Later the doctors said, she had probably died moments after becoming unconscious.

The emotion that was strongest in me when she died and in the weeks immediately following were feelings of relief—relief for both her and me.

She died in January. In April, on Palm Sunday, as the children paraded into and around the sanctuary waving palm branches while the congregation sang a hymn about

Jesus's entry to Jerusalem, I began to cry. Mother loved the Palm Sunday celebration involving children. In my mind I could see her smiling at the children and waving at those she knew. The memory set loose an emotional storm of sorrow. Fortunately I did not have leadership responsibilities in that service for a few minutes and was able to recover from being surprised by my flood of tears before offering the pastoral prayer. It had taken from January to April for my memory of the last two years of her life to recede. I did not miss the woman who had been eighty-four and eighty-five years old. I missed my mother who had been eighty-three and younger. As the memories of my mother eighty-three and younger began to dominate my heart, my sorrow became more intense.

Sometimes the storm of emotion that comes in grief is delayed. I remember a woman who came to see me saying, "I think I am losing my mind. Bob died more than eighteen months ago; I hardly shed a tear until recently. Now I am crying all the time. I can't seem to stop."

Bob had been her husband for more than fifty years. I asked, "Is the Bob you are missing the one who had Alzheimer's for ten years?"

"Oh, no," she said. "I am remembering the years before and I just cannot seem to stop crying."

It had taken eighteen months for the ordeal of Bob's last ten years to fade, before the memories of the other years of their marriage could claim her attention and impact her feelings.

Maria had a similar experience. Maria's husband, Hector, was killed in Iraq as he tried to help rescue a wounded comrade. He had literally given his life trying to save someone else. Maria's grief was both soothed and made more complex by the pride she experienced. She knew Hector was a good man and was not surprised that he would sacrifice himself trying to save someone. Her friends related to the military reinforced her pride by talking about how much they admired him and what he had done. Hector was posthumously awarded a medal for bravery. And in a way Maria was also honored in the way people treated her for the sacrifice that had been forced on her.

But after a while, the power of the story about Hector's sacrifice was no longer soothing. Her friends were moving on with their lives, and Maria missed him. As the full awareness of living the remainder of her life without Hector sank in—her heart was flooded with the anguish of deep and unrelenting sorrow.

Varieties of Storms

The intense phase of sorrow comes in different ways and at different times for different individuals. And when this phase comes, there is no one way the emotion of sorrow is expressed.

Some of us reach out to be held while we weep. Others of us seek solitude for the shedding of tears. Some of us cry like a baby in pain. Others of us sob softly like a child who is lost and afraid. The weeping of some is as silent as a rock, and only the flow of tears tells others of the anguish. Some of us talk to ourselves. Others of us cry out to the one who is dead. Still others of us talk to friends, our words tumbling over one another as if projected outward by some powerful inner pressure. Others of us sit in silence. There is no one way we give vent to our feelings of sorrow.

It is normal to feel the pain of sorrow, and it is healthy to give these feelings some form of expression. In fact it is dangerous to try to deny them. Our feelings are a powerful part of us. When we attempt to deny the reality of our feelings by trying to keep them bottled up, we often discover our unexpressed feelings are shaping all that we think and say and do. Thus, the attempt to control our feelings by denying them, more often than not results in our feelings controlling us.

Unfortunately, many persons in our culture try to hide or deny the emotional storms in their grief. We are encouraged in this denial by our society's tendency to deny sadness, death, and weakness.

The Temptation to Deny Sadness

One of the ways we are encouraged to deny our sorrow is the attitude that happiness is good but that sadness is bad. This is the undercurrent theme in many advertisements. The goal in life for many persons is the pursuit of a happiness in which no sadness can be found. They want to avoid sadness, and they tempt us to hide our sorrow. Persons who tend to equate "feeling happy" with being emotionally healthy have a tendency to deny their sadness and often have difficulty dealing with sadness in others. They are impatient for those who are sad "to get over it." Though these people do not intend to hurt us, their discomfort with sorrow may encourage us to try to deny the sorrow in our grief, or may cause us to feel "bad" because we are feeling sad.

The Temptation to Deny Death

Another attitude that encourages us to keep our emotional storm bottled inside ourselves is our culture's tendency to deny death. Our culture tends to view life as if it were a melodrama in which the hero (or the cavalry) rides in for the rescue just before all is lost. But the truth of the matter is that life is all too frequently more of a tragedy than a melodrama. Our denial of the tragic reality of much in life makes it difficult for us to deal with terminal illness and often tempts both the one who is dying and those who stand by to pretend good health is just around the corner. More often than not, in my experience, the one who is dying knows it and plays along rather than cause discomfort to those closest to him or her. The result is those who stand by the bed miss an opportunity for sharing in one of life's most profound experiences—to say nothing of missing the opportunity to say whatever needs to be said before death comes. This difficulty in facing the reality of death also contributes to the terminally ill facing their death in profound loneliness.

In some ways our denial of the process of dying as well as the reality of death itself is a reflection of one of the strengths within our culture. We are known for our optimism, our unwillingness to admit defeat. This is a great strength and one we need to hold. It is the strength of hope and confidence.

But this hope and confidence needs to come to terms with reality. There is a tendency in our society for us to use the attitude of optimism to hide from realities that frighten us. We dream that if we keep "the right thought," the disturbing reality will go away. This denial of disturbing realities is neither confidence nor hope; it is escapism. We so want life to be the way we want it to be that it is not unusual for some in our society to experience significant anger toward those who bring news that shatters their illusions. This superficial optimism within our culture tempts us to deny any final frustrations—especially the final frustrations of death.

Many in our society refuse to think or talk about death. It is as if we believe death will go away if we ignore it. This attitude toward death encourages us to deny our grief.

Even within our churches we sometimes deny death. For example, in some Protestant churches, the people go straight from Palm Sunday celebrations of triumph to celebrations of the greater triumph in Easter; they tend to give little more than a passing glance to the reality described in the Apostles' Creed: "he was crucified, dead and buried . . ." Some of us can be in such a hurry to be assured of our immortality that we run past the reality of death.

Those who cannot come to terms with the reality of death are tempted to jump too quickly to proclaim what they have only half-heard in churches. Then (conveniently overlooking much that is written in the New Testament) they speak to themselves as much as to us who are in grief saying, "Oh, don't grieve. He is not really dead." I have even heard some try to offer comfort saying, "You should be happy. Now he (or she) is with the Lord in heaven."

However, rather than helping us deal with our grief, such comments encourage us to deny our grief, to hide it, or "get over it." The denial or avoidance of the reality of death makes it more difficult to deal with the experience of grief.

If those around us have trouble dealing with the reality of death, they will probably have trouble dealing with the reality of our grief. Our grief may make them uncomfortable because it confronts them with the reality of death, and they do not want to die. They do not want anyone to die. They want death to go away.

But death is an inevitable reality in life. If we live any significant length of time, death will come to someone we love, and we will experience grief. Death and grief are part of what happens in life.

The Temptation to Deny Weakness

Not only do we have forces or attitudes at work in our society (denial of sadness and denial of death) tempting us to deny or hide our emotional storms, but we also have an inner force at work. This inner force has to do with the fear of showing weakness. Many of us try to avoid admitting our need or dependence on others. We are afraid of showing what some call "signs of weakness."

This fear of appearing weak causes many to hide their feelings. They are afraid of appearing to be "too emotional." Because they view crying as a sign of weakness, they try to "be strong" and not cry. It is this perception of tears that is probably behind the habit of describing someone who is crying as "breaking down." To call crying "breaking down" is to imply something negative about weeping. Rather than to break down, many persons go through life with throats made sore from choking back their tears, trying to deny their sorrow.

Tears Are Okay

Tears are okay. They are not a sign of weakness. David wept. Jesus wept.

Jesus wept at the death of Lazarus (Luke 11:35). His tears were signs of his love—both his love for Lazarus and his love for the family and friends of Lazarus. Love is not a weakness; love is a strength. Love empowers living with healthy vitality. Jesus wept out of the strength of his love, not out of some weakness. He loved. He cared. He was troubled and his spirit was deeply moved. He did not try to hide his feelings. The Son of God revealed his vulnerability to being hurt. He revealed his love.

One of the ways to view our grief is to see it as the reaction of love to loss.

The tears of King David, in the Old Testament, have an added dimension. It is the added dimension of profound disappointment. His son, Absalom, had tried to overthrow David and his government. Yet, David loved his son. He undoubtedly had dreams for Absalom and for their relationship, but Absalom rejected his father and his father's dreams. He led a rebellion against his father, and Absalom was killed. David grieved for all he lost. David grieved over the loss of his son; he grieved over the loss of his dreams for his son, and he grieved the loss of any possibility for reconciliation with his son: "O Absalom, my son, my son!" (2 Samuel 18:33).

Sorrow Is a Sign of Love

Sorrow in our grief is a sign of our love. We weep because a relationship that nourished our lives has ended. We weep because a person who enabled us to feel needed no longer needs us—at least not in the ways we had been needed. We weep because the potential we saw in that relationship died when the person died. We weep because the reconciliation we longed for is no longer possible. All these—being nourished, being needed, seeing potential, longing for reconciliation—are dimensions of love and any or all of them can be the catalyst for our sorrow. If we had no love, we would have no sorrow. To deny our sorrow is to deny our love.

Sorrow Is a Sign of Our Humanity

Our sorrow is also a sign of our humanity, part of the pain that comes when we must deal with a loss that is to us significant. Such sorrow is not merely an adult experience related to the death of someone dearly loved. We form attachments to dreams, goals, relationships, pets, even to things. And when these are lost, are destroyed, or die, we are sad. This is not just an adult experience. Little children cry when the toy they love is lost or because it is broken or because the desired toy is denied.

When some loss triggers a response of sorrow, our humanity—our vulnerability—is exposed. Like the little boy who has lost what he holds dear, we discover ourselves in need of comfort, that is, in need of strength to face what must be faced and the power to move on.

To try to hide (deny) the pain in our grief is for us to try to hide (deny) our humanity. All of us are children. All of us are vulnerable. Yet there is something within us that makes us want to deny vulnerability. We want to hide our hurts. When I have caught myself denying my sorrow, more often than not it is because I am too proud to face—much less admit—my humanity.

The Danger

Some persons will say, "But we do not want to indulge in excessive emotionalism. We do not want to fall into self-pity." Self-pity may be a problem for some, but we who use these statements to justify the denial of our feelings of sorrow are hardly in danger of excessive emotionalism. The danger we are in is the danger that comes from hiding our true feelings. When we hide our true feelings, we cut ourselves off from significant relationships; we block our ability to receive and give love.

Being Open to Grace

God made us human beings capable of love, and this means we are capable of grief that includes sorrow. But God also provides us with the grace we need to deal with the pain in our loss. However, as long as we try to pretend we are self-sufficient, it will be difficult for us to receive the grace God is offering.

In our self-sufficiency we shut the door on other people; and when we shut the door on other people, we shut the door on God's grace, because God's grace usually comes to us through the words and deeds of others. If we focus on trying to prove to ourselves and others that we are so strong that we need no one, we will cut ourselves off from the grace that is offered. In our pride we will have blocked our access to the love we need.

God's grace is most effective in our lives when we do not play games with ourselves or with God. God's love is always reaching out to us, but if we are unwilling to admit our hurts and needs, we are turning our back on God's outstretched arms.

When we do not try to hide our feelings from ourselves or from our friends, we are more likely to be aware of our inadequacies. Aware of our need, we are more likely to be open to love from others, and God's grace that flows through their compassion. Our willingness to admit our heartache and need puts us in a position to be open to the ways God's grace comes into our lives.

4 *Feeling So Alone*

How can we endure the terrible loneliness that is part of our grief? How do we who have deeply enjoyed interdependence survive when a death thrusts us into the lonely position of independence?

Three Lonely Individuals

Ellen

Ellen had enjoyed the bridge party. She was humming as she came into the bedroom, wondering what would be on the TV this late at night. She took off her necklace and was placing it in her jewelry box when she noticed a ring she had not worn in a long time. He had given it to her on a vacation several years ago. A "just-because" gift he had called it. From then on, "just-because" was one of the ways they said, "I love you."

The feeling of loneliness hit her so hard and so suddenly that for a moment she could only stand silently with her eyes closed. She felt incomplete and as alone as if she had been set adrift on vast, empty ocean. Once again she was overwhelmed with the awareness that he was dead and no longer there to hold her and be held by her, to talk to and listen to. It had taken only a moment for the warm afterglow of the bridge party to evaporate and be replaced by the terrible emptiness of her loneliness.

Eugene

Martha and Eugene had what they considered to be a good marriage. They had developed a teamwork pattern of living over the years. Eugene did not realize how much he relied on Martha until she was dead.

It was not the functional dependence that surprised him. He knew there would be a big adjustment regarding keeping house, preparing food, and taking care of his clothes. What he missed most was her friendship. He was not surprised that he missed it, and yet he was surprised to discover how much he had come to rely on her friendship.

He had not realized how vital she was to his decision-making. Over the years he had developed the habit of talking with Martha about everything—major vocational decisions as well as less crucial decisions such as whether or not to buy a new sport coat.

He missed this most. He missed having someone to talk with about the routine and special decisions in living. Since her death, choices—even simple choices—triggered the empty ache of loneliness.

Ruth

Ruth and her husband grew up in an era and in a culture that clearly defined what was "man's work" and what was "woman's work." Because they shared this common background, and because they loved each other very much, they were happily married for fifty-one years.

Both Bill and Ruth assumed one of the ways a man showed he was a man was to "take care of" his wife; this included taking care of all the family's business matters. Therefore it is not surprising that before Bill's death, Ruth had never dealt with insurance or bank statements. She had not dealt with mechanics or repairmen. The largest check she had ever written was for groceries.

When Bill died, Ruth felt very alone, and in her loneliness she felt very vulnerable. Her common sense and her self-confidence told her that she could figure out how to do what needed to be done, but inwardly she longed for him to be there to "take care of" her. Her loneliness for his companionship was intensified by her dependence on him for so many practical matters of daily living.

Loneliness and Our Basic Aloneness

The more we relied on the person who is dead, the more intense our feelings of loneliness are. The lonelier we feel, the more clearly we are able to see the aloneness of our human condition.

There is a sense in which we humans are very much alone. Each of us is a unique person. No one has ever been who we are. No one has ever seen or felt or thought exactly what we have seen, felt, and thought. No other human being can ever know our inmost self. Because each of us is so unique—so special—each of us is somewhat isolated. To some extent aloneness is a basic fact of life. As separate, unique individuals, we can never fully understand one another; we can never be totally sure we know what another person is feeling or thinking. No one can know precisely what we are experiencing in our grief.

In grief we tend to be more keenly aware of our loneliness, and the lyrics of the old folksong become hauntingly meaningful:

> You've got to walk that lonesome valley;
>
> you've got to walk it by yourself.
>
> Nobody else can walk it for you.
>
> You've got to walk it by yourself.[1]

Our feelings of loneliness can be so intense that we are tempted to believe, not only does no one know what we are experiencing, but no one cares. We see our friends in their daily activities and we say to ourselves: "They don't really care. If they really cared, they would show it more." From this position of self-pity our feelings of loneliness can drift into being the way we view our lives. When this happens, we tend to stop reaching out to other people. We say, "Well, if they don't care any more than that, I'm not going to bother with them either."

Fellowship Is Also Real

The biggest danger in this type of self-pity is that we will withdraw from other people. It is dangerous to stop reaching out to others. If we isolate ourselves, the only dimension of life we are able to experience is the lonely

---

1. A traditional American gospel song.

dimension. Then we cut ourselves off from fellowship, and fellowship is a fundamental resource for healthy living.

Although each of us is an individual, we have been created to live together. Each of us is unique with gifts to offer others, and each of us is also a social creature who needs what others have to offer us. God created us to be interdependent. We have been made for community, not solitary confinement.

The reality of our dependence on one another is just as powerful as the counterreality of our basic aloneness or independence. We need to accept both our independence and our need for community in order to be whole. It is through community—through other people—that God nourishes and sustains us. To withdraw from other people is to withdraw from one of the primary settings God uses to give us the grace we need.

Our Choice

We dare not allow the pain of our loneliness to lure us into withdrawing from other people. When someone we dearly love dies, our choice is not whether or not we will be lonely. Our choice is whether we will surrender to our loneliness and live in the self-imposed isolation of withdrawal, or instead choose to pick up our cross of loneliness and reach out to others.

The Greek word for *cross* literally refers to an upright stake or pole. That Greek word referred to the instrument of torturous execution, a large stake sunk vertically in the ground and a crosspiece could be placed on the top to give it the shape of a *T*. But this Greek word we translate as *cross* can also refer to the kind of stake that holds an animal or a tent in place.[2]

The primary meaning of "pick up your cross" has been to willingly accept the cost of discipleship. It has also been understood to mean that we are to pick up the burdens we must bear.

But I am convinced there is another layer of meaning in phrase "pick up your cross/your stake." We are to pick up the stake to which we are tied and move on. Trusting God's grace to see us through, we are to let go of whatever is holding us back from living as God intends and move on.

We dare not surrender to our loneliness, and yet the loneliness in grief can be very painful. It can cause us to feel so empty, so helpless, so isolated, so defeated, that we are tempted to despair. Loneliness can cause us to feel that God has abandoned us, to cry out as Jesus did from the cross: "My God, my God, why hast thou forsaken me?" (Mark 15:34b). Although we see the kind gestures other people are making, and perhaps we even see some of the ways we are needed, the pain of our loneliness seems to drain us of the desire to keep going.

"Pick up the loneliness that is tying you down and move on" is part of what the gospel tells us. This is not to deny the loneliness we experience, but it is to refuse to allow our feeling lonely to tie us down and hold us back from living as God intends.

2. Pierson Parker, "Cross," in *The Interpreter's Dictionary of the Bible*, ed. George Arthur Buttrick (New York: Abingdon, 1962), 1:745.

A Message from Our Heritage

In these moments another aspect of the gospel we need to hear is a message we do not want addressed to us personally. It is both stark and simple. We prefer not to hear it because we want to be rescued from pain and the first part of the message is, "Suffering is part of life."

Only someone who knows little of real suffering glorifies tales about suffering. Typically it is only those who have never been in the hell of battle who enjoy gory war movies. It is those who have not yet experienced real suffering who can casually speak of suffering. Those who know suffering seldom want to talk about it with others.

Jesus clearly understood suffering is part of life. And while his physical suffering was extreme, his suffering was more than physical anguish. He also experienced terrible loneliness. He saw those with whom he had invested so much, turn and run. Even the one who had first realized the significance of his mission (the one he named Peter) denied knowing him. On that terrible Friday, viewing the cross through human eyes, it appeared that Jesus' ministry was a failure. Even Jesus cried out: "My God, my God, why hast thou forsaken me?" (Matthew 27:47). Jesus knew the pain of loneliness, and he experienced the harsh reality of the first part of the message: "Suffering is part of life."

The second part of the message from our Christian heritage is, "God was in Christ"; God—the Source of all that is—*chose* to experience what we experience, to endure what we endure. Through the mystery of the incarnation, God knows our suffering from personal experience. God knows firsthand what it is to be terribly alone and lonely. God in Christ has been through what we go through.

The third part of the message from our heritage is also difficult to communicate because it demands such a leap of faith. The message is, God who was in Christ will give us what we need. The One who seemed so far away when Jesus cried, "Why have you forsaken me?" was really there. God was there enabling Jesus to endure even in the terrible loneliness expressed in his crying out. God had not abandoned Jesus. The confirmation of this was God's victory over the crucifixion. This victory is not merely Jesus' victory; through him it is ours also. This is why Easter is such a big celebration for the people of faith. Through faith we know that the worst that happens cannot finally defeat God, and because by faith we know God is with us, we are not defeated either.

However, just as Jesus was not rescued from his cross, we need not expect to be rescued from ours. But just as Jesus was not defeated by his cross, we need not be defeated by ours either. The One who gave Jesus what he needed in his ordeal will give us what we need in ours.

Suffering is part of life. There are some lonesome valleys each of us must walk, and no one can walk them for us. This is the way life is. God knows this. From firsthand experience, God knows this; God was in Christ. Therefore we are not without hope. Jesus has walked where we walk, and the One who enabled him will enable us.

5 *Handling Grief's Physical Impact*

Accidents

Grief has physical implications. For example, persons in grief are vulnerable to accidents.

I assume most drivers have experienced what I have. Sometimes when I have driven from Austin to San Antonio I have been so busy thinking about some responsibility I have or a conversation I have had that I will wonder whether or not I have gone through San Marcos only to discover from a mileage marker that San Marcos is several miles behind me. I think what allows this to happen is that there is some sort of "automatic pilot" in my brain that allows me to multitask.

When we are experiencing the stress caused by grief, multitasking is not wise. My guess is that whatever functions like an "automatic pilot" in our brain allowing us to multitask, malfunctions in times of stress.

This may explain why it is not unusual for persons to have more accidents while they are in the midst of grief than at other times in their lives. They miss the step on the stair they have never missed before. They have fender benders or worse after years of driving without an accident. They forget the pan is hot and burn their hand, something they had never done before.

One of the ways grief impacts us is that when we are in grief we tend to be more vulnerable to accidents.

When we are in grief (or experiencing significant stress from some other cause), it is wise for us to avoid multitasking and do one thing at a time. When we drive to grocery store, to focus on driving to the grocery store and not multitask on the way. When we come down the stairs, to focus on coming down the stairs and not multitask on the way.

Personally, I find this difficult to do. I am often busy thinking about "this" while doing "that" on my way to "somewhere else." But in times of stress, such as grief, I have found such multitasking to be unsafe.

A Two-Way Street

Accidents are not the only potential physical problem in grief. I suspect most of us have heard someone say, "He grieved himself sick." "She died of a broken heart." There is some basis for folk observations such as these. We are unified human beings; our bodies are not isolated from our emotions. The condition of our bodies can influence how we cope with our emotions; it can even influence the emotions we experience. Our emotional condition can influence our physical health. It is a two-way street.

A pastor was talking with a colleague: "I have noticed that it is not unusual for persons who have been in grief for some time to become so sick that they have to be placed in a hospital."

Some weeks after his wife had died, her husband said: "I'm not hungry. Since she died, I just do not have an appetite."

A father who had buried his son the month before said, "I don't know how long it has been since I really slept. Oh, I sleep but it is a restless sleep. I am up and down all night. When I am asleep I dream and dream. When I wake, I do not feel rested."

In the remainder of this chapter I want us to look at how grief can have a negative impact on our eating, resting, and exercise. Second, I want to examine how these three deficiencies can become a destructive spiral. Third, I will describe some of the ways God's grace is related to this aspect of grief.

Loss of Appetite

Many persons lose their appetites in periods of grief. I think it is possible that this loss of appetite during grief is the body's way of helping us avoid feelings of painful loneliness.

Bill and Louise had been best friends as well as husband and wife. Mealtime was not just a time to eat; for them it was a time to enjoy being with one another and talking about the events of the day, sharing concerns about the children, remembering past experiences, discussing the next trip they would take. Several months after Bill died, Louise became so run-down that she became ill and had to be hospitalized. Her daughter had been concerned for sometime about her mother's loss of appetite. "I'm just not hungry," Louise would say.

When a relationship has been broken by death, I suspect the loss of appetite may be a subconscious way of avoiding the painful loneliness of sitting down to eat alone. As long as we are not hungry, we do not need to sit alone at the kitchen table and awaken our sense of loneliness and be made aware once again of how much we have lost.

For some the loss of appetite may be related to their diminished will to live. The person who died was so important to them that the one in grief no longer has a desire to continue. I have noticed this among some older persons who have lost their spouses. It surfaces in comments such as, "I just don't want to go on without her."

Some combination of these reasons could be why some people experiencing intense grief lose their appetite. Of course, the loss of appetite might be some other reason entirely, but regardless of the precise cause, if one does not eat properly, physical health will deteriorate.

Loss of Sleep

Some people in the emotional stress of grief have difficulty sleeping.

For example, Roger and Marie had shared a bed for forty-seven years. When Roger died, Marie found herself dreading to go to bed at night. The bed seemed so empty. Its emptiness reminded her of all she had lost. Perhaps it was this dread of a lonely bedroom that influenced her to believe she did not feel sleepy and to avoid the bedroom as long as possible.

For some, the difficulty of going to sleep is related to some unrecognized fear of death. Others may be so worried about how they are going to face the future without this person on whom they had relied so heavily, that when they try to go to sleep their minds raise one potential problem after another. Instead of sleeping, they lie in bed worrying.

It is not unusual for persons who are in grief to dream more than they normally do. Sometimes this dreaming can contribute to restless sleep. If the dreams are unpleasant, those in grief may begin avoiding going to bed. They will try to get by on as little sleep as possible. This was my experience in the weeks following my father's death. I would wake, aware I had had a terrible dream although I could not recall the details. The dreams were so disturbing I found myself delaying going to sleep.

When any of us does not get enough rest, our bodies become run-down, and our resistance to disease is lowered. Also our ability to cope emotionally is undercut by sleep deprivation. Then, our physical problems add to our emotional problems that in turn add to our physical problems.

Lack of Exercise

In grief, physical exercise is often neglected. Other concerns have our attention, or we say we do not feel like exercising. Sometimes grief tempts us to "give up" and face each day with an attitude of "Why bother anymore?" This attitude undercuts our motivation to remain physically active. A lack of exercise can cause us to be sluggish. It can also contribute to our loss of appetite and our inability to rest.

Grief and Health Problems

It is not surprising that some persons in grief become physically ill within a few months after the loss of someone they dearly loved. Having neglected food, sleep, and exercise they become run-down and an easy victim for the first disease that comes along. This happened to both my mother and my mother-in-law in the months following the deaths of their husbands.

The loss of physical health can also add to the emotional stress in grief. When we are in poor physical health, we tend to be less able to cope effectively with our emotional challenges. In fact, poor physical health may be a significant factor in experiencing an increase in emotional problems.

A Destructive Spiral

When our bodies are in poor condition, our ability to cope with our emotional anguish is diminished. Less able to cope with emotional stress, we are tempted more than ever to stop living. Any reduction in our will to live only compounds our eating, sleeping, and exercise problems. And so, a destructive spiral is set in motion. This spiral can lead only to illness if it is allowed to continue.

It is not physical health alone that is harmed by inadequate eating, sleeping, and exercising. When I was a young adult, I experienced significant depression and a major factor was my poor diet, inadequate sleep, and lack of exercise. The sorrow in grief can stimulate feelings of depression, and when these are compounded by failure to eat right, sleep, and exercise, the depression that is a normal part of the grief process can become more intense. Sometimes prolonged depression is a symptom that the biochemical system has been thrown out of balance. When this happens medical help is essential for regaining emotional as well as physical health.

Grace in This Situation

How does grace come to us in this situation? It comes in all the ways we are reminded about the gift of life and the responsibility of living. God's grace comes through those people who encourage us to eat balanced meals and to be as physically active as we are able. It comes through all those persons, insights and events that reveal to us we are in some way needed. It comes through doctors and medicine, which assist in regaining emotional and physical health.

The temptation to quit can be very strong. When we are tempted to give up and withdraw is the when we especially need to seek resources outside ourselves. When I have been low, I have found that I need to turn to others as a way of seeking God's grace. If I was left to myself, alone in those low moments, my prayers tended to be various ways of saying: "Poor me." When I have reached out to others, sharing my feelings, I have discovered help. What I am unable to receive from God in private because of my emotional state, I have discovered I have a better chance of receiving through others.

When our sorrow and sense of loss drains our will to move on, we need to receive God's grace. The way this gift comes into our lives may or may not involve traditional "church talk," but God's grace is not limited to using the language and metaphors of Christianity. However we experience the grace of God in our lives, the end result will be that eventually we will recover (or discover) a sense of hope and the will to move on, even after we have experienced the worst that life brings.

Jesus said there is comfort for those who mourn (Matthew 5:4). For those in grief (those who mourn) there is strength to face life as it is, and also the power to move on. Being strengthened and empowered to deal with the bad times is the essence of "being comforted." Jesus pointed the way to strength for facing life and the power for moving on.

We humans have a tendency to focus only on ourselves. This can be especially true when we are in the grips of sorrow and a sense of loss. But Jesus warned us that to focus only on ourselves is destructive (Luke 9:24).

He showed us that abundant life (life with an eternal quality to it) comes from our focusing on the will of God and on the needs of our neighbors. He talked about it in terms of living a life of love—loving God and neighbor.

If we focus only on our grief (*only* on our sorrow and our loss) we will bog down in our grief like someone caught in quicksand. But if we look beyond ourselves, there is hope. God's purpose for each of us is more than a self-serving existence. In the midst of our sorrow and loss, God's gift is more than not experiencing any heartache.

God's purpose for Jesus was certainly more than for Jesus always to be comfortable. Jesus was more important than that, and so are we. It is clear in what Jesus said and did that we have been created for the purpose of living in harmony with God, living as God intends; our words and deeds are to be shaped by our love of God and neighbor as well as by love for ourselves.

When we begin to sense this God-given purpose, this sense of purpose gives rise to our living with hope; and with hope, we rediscover and recover our will to live. As our will to live and move on with our lives increases, we begin to regain our physical and emotional health.

6 *Dealing with Anger*

It is not unusual for grief to express itself through anger.

Anger toward the Dead

No one was in the cemetery except Sandra. She came to see if the gravestone had been delivered. It had not; there was only the little metal marker stating his name and the dates of his birth and death. It was the lonely decoration on the grave; all the funeral flowers had dried and been thrown away.

Sandra stood looking down at the bare dirt mound of her husband's grave. She was alone in the cemetery. A mocking bird was going through his routine of songs; but she did not notice. Nor was she aware of the occasional truck or car that sped past on the highway just beyond the cemetery gate.

"Why?" It was spoken with angry intensity. "Why did you die and leave me all alone?" Her tears were as much of anger as of sorrow. "Why did you leave me with so much unfinished? How dare you to die with the business in such a mess and the kids only half grown. Oh, I know you did not choose to have cancer. But when you knew death was a very real probability, why didn't you at least try to get your business affairs in order? People say they are sorry you died. Well, I'm sorry I am alive. I wish all this was your problem now instead of mine. You could have made all this easier on us; you really could. But you didn't; you wasted precious time, and now I have to try to make sense of the mess you left, and I have no real experience for that."

Sandra's fists clinched. Her body was tense and shaking. "What am I going to do? What am I going to do?"

The hurt and fears that are part of grief frequently set loose feelings of anger, and occasionally the anger is focused on the person who died.

Louis was certainly aware of his anger toward his brother, Fred. Fred had committed suicide, and done it in such a way that their father would be the one to find him. Louis dearly loved Fred. He knew Fred had been struggling with severe depression for at least three years and was seeing a psychiatrist regularly. Louis had done all he could to make Fred promise to call him whenever he felt like hurting himself. But Fred had not called. Fred had gone out in the backyard and hung himself from the big oak tree. Louis felt some sympathy for the kind of internal anguish that had motivated Fred to this drastic mode of relief, but he was also very angry. "You thought only of yourself and obviously did not care what your suicide would do to us."

Anger toward the one who died is not unusual, especially when the death is a suicide.

Marie looked at the picture of her young husband; he was in the army uniform he loved to wear. He was handsome and smiling. She loved him and missed him, but she was angry at him. He did not have to go back. His tour of duty was over. He could have gotten out of the army. She begged him not to reenlist, but he felt he had a duty to his comrades who were carrying the load. He said he had to reenlist in order to be able to live with himself. She had argued with him about his responsibility to their two young children, if not to her. But he was determined. Now her worst fear had been realized, and she was angry that he had chosen to take that risk, leaving her with two small children to rear. She could no longer focus primarily on being their mother; now she had to find a job outside the home in order to feed, clothe, and house her children and herself. To make matters worse, she had limited formal education and job experience. She was scared, and she was angry. "You and your precious duty to your comrades. What about your duties as father and husband?"

Anger toward the one who died is not unusual, especially when the death was caused by risks we had urged that person not to take.

Anger toward God

Sometimes our grief expresses itself in anger toward God. This happens often in the grief that follows the death of a young person.

Paul was only nineteen when he died. He had his whole adult life yet to live. Paul was bright; he had many talents. It seemed he had a great future ahead of him. But his sore leg had been more than a bruise. It had been a symptom of a fatal form of advanced bone cancer.

"I thought God was supposed to be a God of love," said one of his friends. "There may be a God, but after what has happened to Paul, I do not see how anyone can recite that stuff about how much God loves us. And all that other junk about our loving God, after all this, it's worse than nonsense. How dare anyone tell me I am supposed to love God after God let this happen to Paul."

When Sally and Roger put Lucy, their infant daughter, to bed, they felt a wonderful joy, watching her tiny arms wave. They wound up the music box, turned on the night light and turned off the ceiling light. Then they went in the den to watch TV. Sometime later, they went to check on Lucy and found she had died in her sleep.

"Why?" There was no answer to be given. Had they done something wrong? Had they failed to take some precaution? "No," the doctor told them; "We just do not know much about this sort of death. It is rare among infants, but it does happen."

As Roger moved on with his life, he was angry at God. Was God so inept a creator as to have such a flaw in his design? Was God a capricious deity? Or was God simply an impersonal force as uncaring as gravity?

Anger toward God can be part of grief. Often anger surfaces when the one who died was young and the death appears to be of what we call "natural causes."

Anger toward the Living

Not only can grief sometimes cause us to be angry toward the person who died and/or toward God, but our grief sometimes explodes in anger toward friends or family members.

Carol was helping her mother clean out her father's closet and workroom. It was one of those necessary ordeals that follow the funeral. Carol sorted the items to discover what should be thrown away, what should be given away, and what should be kept.

"What do you mean, throwing away these papers?" Anger was in her mother's voice. "Your father worked hard on this material. How dare you throw it away! I thought you loved your father more than that."

"But, Mother, what good are these papers to us? We can't keep everything."

"These papers were important to your father; we just can't throw them away. It would be like throwing him away. It is bad enough for him to be dead without his own flesh and blood treating his work like garbage."

Anger is a powerful reality in our lives. It can be set loose by a death. When someone we love dies, we are hurt. It is not unusual to feel that the timing of the death (if not the death itself) is unfair. On top of this, death sometimes thrusts problems and situations on us we would never choose for ourselves. When we have drawn a great deal of security and satisfaction from a relationship, we can feel robbed when the other person dies.

I have noticed that it is not unusual for persons in grief to be more sensitive than they normally are (whatever is normal for them). Words and deeds that in other times would not have bothered them, in the midst of their grief become the catalyst that sets loose feelings of anger.

The state of their emotions is something like a physical bruise. If I have a painful bruise on my shoulder, and you greet me by slapping me on that shoulder, I will flinch. "That should not cause you to flinch; I did not hit you that hard," you might tell me. But under my shirt is the bruise you do not see, and the slightest pressure on that bruise is painful. Your telling me not to flinch is wasted breath.

Telling people in the midst of grief they should not get upset about "this" or "that" is like telling a bruised person that he or she should not flinch when the bruise is hit. Grief can cause us to be more emotionally sensitive than we normally are. This means that when we are in grief, we are more likely to become angry in situations that normally would not have bothered us. And it is not unusual for situations that would have bothered us before we were in grief to arouse within us anger more intense than is appropriate.

I have also noticed this anger is more often expressed to family members or strangers than to colleagues or friends. My hunch is this is because we are less guarded with strangers and family members. Of course, when one grief-bruised family member explodes in anger to another grief-bruised family member, the result can be an ugly emotional collision.

I know of no way to prevent the emotional bruising that comes with intense grief. However, when we are aware that emotional bruising is part of intense grief, then a willingness to forgive oneself and others, accompanied by a good sense of humor, can help see us through.

Sometimes anger in the midst of grief is both triggered and intensified by a lack of knowledge and by fear. This was true for Emily. She was only twenty when her husband, was killed in combat, and she received an insurance payment of five hundred thousand dollars. It was more money than anyone in Emily's extended family had ever imagined having. Emily's grief was complicated by relatives advising her about what to do with the money, even though none of them had ever been a steward of such an amount. She began to resent what appeared to her to be excessive interest in the insurance money. The resentment became anger after a cousin with bad credit wanted Emily to help her buy a car, and an uncle tried to talk her into investing the money in a dream he had. The anger was made more intense by her fear that she would be taken advantage of. She was keenly aware of her lack of formal education. It was not long until she would explode in anger when anyone even appeared about to ask what she was going to do. Then Emily would be upset with herself because of her angry reaction.

Grace in Anger

God's grace can use our anger to work toward good. This is clearly evident when our anger is stimulating positive action. For example, anger might be the tool God uses to push Sandra into taking charge of her life in a new way.

"I'm not going to do to our kids what you did to me. I'm not going to leave everything left undone. I'll show you! I'll straighten this mess out yet." Sandra walked away from the grave determined to take charge of her life.

Anger is one of the signals God has given us to alert us that something may be wrong in a relationship. Carol's mother went to her bedroom after her harsh words with her daughter. "Why did I blow up like that? She is only trying to help." Introspection might reveal some fears that need to be faced, or it might expose some unresolved guilt, or it might bring to the surface some conflicts she had with Carol. This revelation makes both resolution of the conflict and reconciliation in the relationship possible. Pain has the potential to move us toward action that leads to healing.

It is the grace of God (whether we are aware of it or not) that empowers us to ask for forgiveness and enables us to accept forgiveness and to offer it to others. Often family members who have forgiven one another discover they are closer than ever.

It is the power of grace at work in anger that draws our attention to aspects of life we have ignored. Paul's friend may discover in his anger toward God that he has not thought much about what he believes. In his angry struggle to relate his understanding of God's love to his view of human suffering, he may discover a more profound belief in God.

Anger can be used by grace as catalyst for some sort of positive action or change. Louis became a volunteer working with organizations trying to reduce the number of teenage suicides. Marie formed a support group to involve other women who had lost their husbands in military action.

Emily was upset with members of her family who tried to tell her what to do with the insurance money. Yet she was also aware of her lack of knowledge about what to do. When some of them expressed their concern about her lack of knowledge and experience with money, Emily's anger was the catalyst that made her decide to seek help. But who could she trust? Then she remembered a high school teacher whom she had respected and with whom she had had a good relationship in high school. Emily phoned Mrs. Etheridge, and that was the beginning of several conversations that helped Emily think through what she needed to do. Also, through Mrs. Etheridge, Emily was put in touch with persons she was confident would be objective and helpful in assisting her discover her options. For Emily, Mrs. Etheridge had been an agent of grace.

Aware of it or not, believe it or not, grace can be at work in our lives, even through our anger.

Anger Can Be Destructive

Anger can be helpful when it is a catalyst for positive change. But, when our anger is not merely part of what we experience, but a reality at work in our lives controlling us, it can hurt us and others. Anger is a powerful emotion—the greater the anger, the greater the potential destructive power.

Anger can evolve into bitterness and resentment. This happens when we focus only on the pain we have endured. When we allow ourselves to dwell on our hurts and the injustices in our lives, our attitude begins to decay. We stop living and growing in grace. Rather than being in control of our anger, our anger and resentment begin to control us. We allow the possibilities the future holds to be banished from our sight by our angry resentment about what others did or did not do. We stop living, and we rot in the resentment that "he" or "she" or "it" ruined our lives.

Resentment and bitterness are tempting because once we place the blame on "X" for our disappointments and unfulfilled dreams, we can live in the illusion that we are not responsible for our lives, saying to ourselves, "After what has happened to me, how else could I be?" Focused on the wounds we have received, we lash out at others; we blame, we attack, we kick, we gripe, we tear down. When we try to excuse ourselves saying: "'X' is to blame for the way I am," the price we pay is distorting our lives with our bitterness, resentment, denial of responsibility for our own behavior. When we blame our faults on others, we tend to drift toward mistrust and cynicism. Then, all too often, what we say and do hurts others; and they, in turn, tend to respond by inflicting some sort of pain on someone else. Like the spoiled apple in the barrel, we spread our decay. Anger can set in motion a destructive chain reaction.

Anger is a powerful reality. It can be a catalyst for positive action, but it can also be a very negative force in our lives.

The Temptation to Deny Anger

Because anger is so powerful, and because it can be so destructive, it is not unusual for some of us try to deny our anger. When we feel that we have been wronged, we sometimes deny ourselves the right to feel angry. But the reality of the anger within does not go away; like a torpedo run amuck, it seeks another target. One of those other targets can be ourselves. All too often, when we deny our anger, the result is we end up in depression. Without real-izing what we have done, we become the object of our own anger. This is when we turn our anger on ourselves and in-appropriately blame ourselves for whatever is wrong. The result is we do not like ourselves and we feel depressed.

If Sandra were to deny her anger toward her husband, it is very possible (even probable) that her denied anger toward her husband would turn inward on herself. "If I had been a better wife, this would not have happened. If I were a better person, all this mess would not bother me." She would lose touch with self-respect and dislike herself for "being so helpless."

If Paul's friend denied his anger toward God, his anger would likely seek another object. It might be aimed at the doctors or at Paul's parents. Or his denied anger might turn inward on himself. It might even take the form of guilt for having lived while his friend died.

If Marie were to deny her anger about her husband reenlisting and being killed, she might be persuaded to believe that she is supposed to be proud rather than angry that her husband died for his country. This double bind of denying anger and feeling it is her duty to feel proud could set her on edge so that even aggravations by her children would trigger excessive anger and inappropriate punishment. Or, her anger might turn into self-contempt and guilt for having been upset about her husband's reenlistment and her failure to be "a good Army wife."

If Carol's mother tried to bottle her fears and angers because her daughter threw away some of her husband's papers, it is very probable that those fears and that anger would turn in on herself. The result would be that she would be captive to the fear that her life did not matter and that not even Carol really cared. "After all, if Carol had no more respect for her father than to throw away his papers, how much less does she respect or care about me?" If this was her response, her bottled feelings would ferment and become even more intense feelings of loneliness and despair.

Anger is a powerful reality. It does not go away by our denying it. More often than not, denied anger turns inward and becomes a form of depression, or it comes out of us like a ricocheting bullet, wounding unfortunate bystanders. We must deal with our anger, or it will deal us more misery while at the same time spreading the consequences of our misery to others.

The Gospel and Anger

When our grief expresses itself in anger, what does the Gospel offer us? What are some of the expressions of God's grace that relate to the anger in our grief?

Earlier we noticed that anger can be a catalyst for positive change. The push anger gives us is sometimes the shove we need to begin working to make life better for ourselves and others. Sometimes it takes a burst of anger to help us discern a need in the world around us and set us to doing what we are able to do to address that need.

Anger—A Gift For Relationships

Anger can be a good gift to help us in our relationships with other persons. It is one of the brooms God has given us to sweep the harmful behavior out of our relationships. This is easiest to illustrate in a marriage; however, the basic insight is true of all relationships. Marriages seldom fall apart because of a single crisis. More often than not, they fall apart because of "the last straw." When I have heard an angry spouse say, "That was the last straw," in my imagination I see a wagon loaded with hay on which someone drops one more straw, causing the wagon to fall apart. The reason the marriage wagon falls apart is seldom because of "the last straw," but rather because for too long the wagon has been carrying too heavy a load of "straw," and "the last straw" is merely "*the most recent* straw."

Anger can be understood as a gift God gives us for the purpose of keeping the "straw" from piling up too high on our relationship wagons.

It is like the gift of a good broom. Of course, a broom can be misused. It can be used like a weapon to beat others over the head. However, the possibility of misuse does not change the fact that it is a good gift.

It was helpful for Sandra to work through her anger toward her husband because then she was able to move beyond that anger. When she had worked through her anger, she finally reached the point of being able to forgive him. When she did, many years of good memories surfaced to give her consolation and strength.

God Can Use Our Anger toward Him

The suffering of the innocent or the loss of a life for one who has not reached his or her potential is a terrible mystery with which we have to live. It is not unusual for such tragedy to cause us to be angry with God.

The Gospel tells us that God understands what we are going through; this, in part, is what is revealed in the incarnation. Through Christ God has taken on what it is to be human. God understands and accepts our anger. God's wisdom and love for us is so deep and strong that our anger is neither going to hurt God nor damage God's love for us.

Yet it is not unusual for those of us who have been raised in the church to deny ever being angry with God. Although our anger cannot hurt God, our denying our anger toward God, and our phony faith, can hurt us. Our pretensions do not fool God, but they get in the way of (or even block) a healthy relationship with God. How can God deal with our hostility toward him if we deny it while trying to impress others with our phony piety? How can God deal with our doubts if in our phony faith for public show we deny our doubts? When our energies are consumed by our pretending to love and have faith, we have no energies left to seek or receive the kind of comfort God is trying to give us.

When we are confronted by the terrible mysteries in life, we are placed in a situation analogous to Jacob's (see Genesis 32:24–28). In the midnight hours Jacob wrestled with an angel. If Jacob had walked away from that fight, refusing to wrestle with the angel of God because of some phony, pious excuses, Jacob would not have received God's blessing; he would not have become Israel. But Jacob wrestled, and although the fight changed the way he walked (his hip was thrown out of joint), he was blessed; he became Israel, that is, blessed by God for wrestling with God.

At times we are alone in the darkness of our living, and we have to wrestle with mysteries we cannot comprehend. In these grim ordeals of living, we must be open *with* God in order for us to be open *to* God. The blessing (whatever that is) will come only as we hang on like Jacob and abandon neither our faith nor our integrity.

In order to be open to the blessing God would give us in our new situation, we must be open *with* God—even open about our anger toward God. The gospel assures us that God not only can take our anger but that in our honest struggles of faith He reaches out to us.

God Can Use Our Anger toward Others

But what about the kind of anger Carol's mother expressed? What does the gospel say to that? I have discovered that the root cause of much of my anger is some sort of fear. Her anger was probably an explosion of several fears she had bottled inside herself. The root cause of her anger may have been fear about her ability to cope; or it may have been fear that her own death will wipe away her labors; or perhaps she may have been afraid that if Carol did not see her father's papers as important, Carol might not see her mother's efforts as worth much either. It was probably a combination of several of these fears that was the unrecognized cause of her anger.

The only way to handle fears (as opposed to letting them handle us) is first of all to recognize them. But how do we do this? Our anger is one of the clues we have that point toward what really scares us, because anger is often the first way our fear expresses itself. Trying not to be angry will not be successful if what is behind the anger is some sort of fear. Becoming aware of our anger can be the first step toward identifying our fears so that we can face those fears and deal with them.

In the conversation that might have flowed from the confrontation regarding the papers, Carol's mother might be set on the road to coping with her new situation. This is more likely to happen if Carol's mother is willing to explore why Carol's actions made her angry.

When Anger Is Misused

All this says that anger is a good gift, but implied in this view of anger is the assumption we will use this gift properly. What about our misuses of this gift? What about the times we have used this broom more like a weapon than a tool? What does the gospel offer us who have misused the anger in our grief?

Through the gospel we are given the reality of forgiveness. As was said earlier in this book, forgiveness is something more than merely overlooking events in the past. The forgiveness a parent gives a child is rooted in the parent's awareness of the potential that his or her love senses in the child. And when I, the child, sense that my potential is more important than my past wrongs, I have a new lease on living. Forgiveness is the gift of a new view of the present and the future. To receive forgiveness is to obtain a new perspective on our lives. The past is not forgotten, and the inevitable consequences of the past are not avoided, but there is a new view of what is important. Instead of being dominated by our awareness of the ways we have misused our lives in the past, we are free to focus on the positive possibilities that are before us.

Forgiveness does not undo what we did, nor does it stop the consequences of our deeds. Through forgiveness we see life in a new light. In this new light we accept that what is past is behind us. We no longer live in bondage to our misuses of the past. We may still be paying some of the consequences, but our focus, our attention, is not dominated by the old guilt but by new hope. In this new hope we sense positive possibilities in the present and in the future. We can even sense positive possibilities in the consequences of our wrong deeds. We have been given newness of life. We experience a kind of renewal.

In the awareness of this forgiveness of ourselves, we are able to forgive others. The past hurts others caused us do not evaporate from our memory; some scars may stay with us, but rather than being hung up on past pain, we now focus on new and positive possibilities, both for ourselves and for those who hurt us. This emphasis on new life sets us free from bondage to old resentments and anger. The new perspective we have on our lives spreads to all of our relationships. Those who have received forgiveness, forgive.

Summary

Anger is a powerful reality, and this powerful reality is sometimes part of our grief experience. It is a good gift God has given us as a catalyst to make needed changes. However, we can misuse this gift and discover that in our misuse of anger we have hurt ourselves and others. When this happens, we need to remember another aspect of the gospel, another dimension of God's grace; we need to remember the reality of forgiveness.

7 *Dealing with Regret and Guilt*

Regret

Feeling regret and feeling guilty are somewhat similar, but they are not the same. When we feel guilty we do not like ourselves because of some behavior. Regret does not condemn us the way guilt does. Regret is more like profound disappointment than self-contempt.

Regret is part of all relationships that have any significant length and depth because each of us is imperfect. We say what we wish we had not said. We leave unsaid what we wish we had put into words. We make mistakes and wish we could undo what we have done. We wish we had the chance to do now what we should have done then. Regret is part of life, and it is not unusual for regret to be keenly felt as part of the grief experience.

Sometimes our regret is not related to our behavior as much as it is triggered by our memories of what the one who died did or failed to do, or said or failed to say.

What keeps regret from being guilt or anger is our awareness of the good intentions motivating what was said or done.

"I did the best I could, knowing what I knew then."

"She did the best she knew how to do."

Being aware of the good intentions motivating what was said and done goes a long way toward soothing the hurt and preventing a break in relationship. Then, regret rather than guilt or anger is the by-product of the pain.

When words or deeds (or a lack of them) did some damage or hurt our feelings, it is the grace of God at work in us and through the relationship that enables us discern the good intention motivating what was said and done. It is trusting that good was intended that defuses anger and resentment.

It is grace at work in us that enables us to recognize our error and to be gentle with ourselves, so that what we have to deal with is regret that we did not know better rather than the self-contempt of guilt because of the wrong we chose to do. "I deeply regret what I did (and/or said). I was trying to help, but I made the wrong choice."

Guilt

In the tangle of all we go through in grief, it is not unusual to also have to deal with feelings of guilt. By "feeling guilty," I mean not liking ourselves because we know the pain and problems caused by what we did or failed to do, by what we said or failed to say, were not merely the result of mistakes or innocent ignorance. They were the byproducts of our self-centeredness, greed, or pride—our sin.

Sometimes we have difficulty identifying the behavior causing our guilt feelings because the problem is not merely what we did or failed to do. Our problem is we failed to *be* who we know we should be. We may have done what we were supposed to do, but we did it out of greed or with feelings of resentment, and the result is we do not like ourselves. The aftermath is not merely regret about mistakes but guilt about sin.

We do not like ourselves and in our state of feeling guilty it is difficult for us to believe God or anyone else could love us if he/she really knew us. Feeling guilty we have difficulty accepting or expressing affection. We find ourselves unable to accept the love we need and more than reluctant to offer the love others need from us.

Sources of Feeling Guilty

Some of our guilt feelings are related to something we did (or failed to do) years ago. From time to time these painful memories hinder our ability to be and do our best. In the last chapter, Mary felt guilty when she remembered ways she had hurt her father. The remembering that takes place as part of the grief process, especially the remembering of unpleasant experiences, can awaken and/or intensify our feelings of guilt.

Some of our guilt feelings are not related to what we did and as much as to the low opinion we have of ourselves. Joe did not feel his life was much of a success. He was not sure what "success" was but he felt he had not "made it," and he believed his father had been disappointed in him. When his father died, Joe felt a sense of guilt and self-contempt.

Sometimes the shock of a death and the anguish of grief can release guilt we have repressed. This happened to Nancy. Her best friend, Rachel, died. In the grief that Nancy experienced there were feelings of guilt. At first, Nancy could not figure out why she was feeling guilty. Her friendship with Rachel was almost ideal. One day while watching a soap opera Nancy became aware of the source of her guilt feelings.

Twenty years before Rachel's death, Nancy had had an affair with another friend's husband. That friend found out, and their friendship ended. Nancy was in grief over the loss of both this friend and her lover. She felt guilty because of all the pain she helped create. However, she did not work through her grief and guilt. She had repressed it. All this happened years before Nancy met Rachel. Nancy's grief regarding Rachel's death awakened the feelings of grief and guilt she had repressed twenty years ago. Sometimes the negative feelings deep within us have been waiting a long time for some event to turn them loose.

Sometimes the guilt feelings are more directly related to the death. For example, a twelve-year-old boy accidentally hanged himself. He was standing on a ladder tying a rope to a tree limb. Somehow he knocked the ladder over and became entangled in the rope. He strangled to death. No one knows exactly how it happened. The parents of this boy had strong guilt feelings. The father said, "If only I had not left the ladder in the backyard. If only I had thrown away that old rope." The mother added: "If only I had gone outside a few minutes earlier."

In another situation a father accidentally shot and killed his son. In yet another situation a teenager was driving and had an accident in which his mother was killed. In these and similar situations, the feelings of grief were accompanied by self-accusation and strong feelings of guilt.

Whenever we can see some clear connection between the death and what we did (or failed to do), our grief tends set loose intense feelings of guilt.

Almost thirty years after World War II, a gentle and kind man who was the only survivor of his unit that fought from D-Day until Germany surrendered killed himself. For years he had been under the care of psychiatrists because of his severe depression related to feeling guilty that he had survived when his friends had not. One day he was putting away a gun his son had left out of the gun cabinet that was usually locked. Walking down the hall toward the room where the cabinet was, he shot himself. The family was confident his suicide was not a planned event because he had left food cooking on the stove. The son who had not put the gun away struggled with the self-contempt of guilt. "If only I had put the gun away and locked the cabinet."

It is not unusual for us humans to search for something to feel guilty about. This searching for "what I did wrong" is sometimes related to our fears and doubts about ourselves. It is as if we are looking for something that will confirm our low opinion of ourselves. We are especially vulnerable to such feelings in the wake of unexplainable tragedy.

It is difficult to stand in the wake of a tragedy with all its unanswered questions. It is tempting to believe if we could find some cause, something that went wrong, someone to blame, the tragedy would be more acceptable. It is difficult to live with unanswered questions, especially in regard to tragic deaths. Longing for tragedy to make sense, we will sometimes blame ourselves and assume the burden of guilt rather than deal with the unanswerable questions in tragedy.

A woman whose husband died of a sudden heart attack blamed herself for not having forced him to take better care of himself. A man whose wife died unexpectedly blamed himself: "I should have done something to prevent her death."

Our low opinion of ourselves and our longing for an answer will even tempt us to view our loss as some form of punishment. This was Bill's temptation. His wife died a slow death. She was only twenty-six when she died, and she left Bill with a four-year-old girl. Bill had to struggle with the suspicion that her suffering and death were somehow his fault. He was tempted to believe that his loss and sorrow was some sort of punishment. By assuming the blame there would be an explanation, a reason, and he could view his anguish as punishment. If he assumed the guilt he would not have to cope with the profound mysteries of unexplainable suffering. He was tempted to assume the blame and thus create the illusion of understanding why it had all happened.

In the story of Adam and Eve, God forbids them to eat the fruit of "the tree of the knowledge of good and evil" (Genesis 2–3). In Gerhard von Rad's commentary on the book of Genesis, he states that the phrase "knowledge of good and evil" used in this story is a Hebrew expression that means "knowing everything." Thus the tree was the tree of "knowing everything." In telling them not to eat the fruit of this tree, God was telling Adam and Eve to refrain from trying to be "know-it-alls." God was telling Adam and Eve that they could fulfill their place in the creation only by coming to terms with their human limitations. In God's forbidding them to eat the fruit of that tree, God was warning them that if they tried to be know-it-alls (to live like the Creator rather than living as creatures), it would destroy them.

In the wake of a tragedy (with all its unanswerable questions), we are tempted to assume guilt in order to furnish ourselves with explanations—in order to satisfy our desire to be know-it-alls. When we take on the pain of guilt rather than face the dark, unanswerable mysteries in human suffering, we do what Adam and Eve did; we try to be God, knowing what only God can know.

We have pointed to five sources of guilt: (1) our memories, especially our unpleasant memories; (2) our low opinion of ourselves, which is sometimes coupled with (3) repressed guilt; (4) our seeing some connection between what we did (or failed to do) and the death; and (5) our preference to assume guilt rather than cope with unanswerable mysteries regarding human suffering.

Grace in Discovering the Cause of Feeling Guilty

One of the ways God's grace is at work among us in this phase of our grief is in helping us identify the source of our guilt.

Sometimes merely realizing what is causing us to feel guilty will free us from those negative feelings. This is usually the case when the guilt we feel is an inappropriate guilt that we have been taught to feel. For example, Louise felt guilty after her father died. She did not know why. She guessed it was part of her grief, but that realization did not relieve her from the burden of feeling she had done something wrong.

In a conversation with a friend, the cause of her guilt came out. She was talking about her father's funeral: "Everything was just the way he wanted—except he did not die at home with his family around him. He had often said that is the way he wanted to go. He died with strangers in an intensive-care unit in the hospital."

No sooner had she spoken than she realized his dying away from home was the cause for her feeling she had done something wrong. Obviously she had done nothing wrong. She knew she had done the best she could for her father. The mere awareness of what was causing her guilt feelings released her. She did experience regret that her father's wish had not been fulfilled, but there is a vast difference between regret over someone's wish not coming true and the self-contempt of "It's my fault."

God's grace is at work in all the ways we are helped to identify the source of our guilt feelings. Sometimes identifying the source of our guilt is enough to release us from feeling guilty. More frequently this identification is only the first step toward our accepting forgiveness. This first step is quite a gift. Anyone who has experienced the anguish of seemingly sourceless self-contempt knows just how big a gift it really is. As long as we cannot identify the cause of our guilt feelings, we have little hope of being released from our sense of guilt.

However, most of the time, the knowledge of what is causing us to feel guilty is not merely the identification of the source of our guilt. The writer of Psalm 51 knew what was causing him to feel guilty: "I know my transgression, / and my sin is ever before me" (Psalm 51:3). He knew why he felt guilty and did not like himself. His past haunted him; he could not get away from it. It may be so with us.

When we are bogged down in the awareness that we have failed to be the persons we should have been and do not like ourselves, it is often difficult for us to believe God or anyone who knew the truth about us could love us. Sometimes this self-contempt is so severe that we are tempted to withdraw from the very people who are most likely to be the instruments of God's healing grace.

Grace in Our Yearnings

One of the ways God's grace is at work is in our yearning to be at peace with ourselves, to be in harmony with life, to be able to love, and in longing to be loved. This yearning for wholeness, peace, and fulfillment is a gift God's grace. It is the gift of a door God has given us for his grace to come through. This yearning can motivate us to be open to the ways God's mercy comes into our lives. When our guilt has locked us inside ourselves, God's mercy comes seeking us through the doorway of our deepest yearnings.

Walter felt sick when he remembered what he had done. How could he have allowed himself to cause so much pain? If only there was something he could do! He longed to have the self-respect he had once enjoyed. He longed to be able to look his neighbors in the face without feeling guilty. Finally, he could not keep it all bottled inside himself. His aches and longings drove him to seek some advice from a friend. His yearnings for wholeness and peace sent him outside himself. Through their ongoing conversations, Walter was confronted by mercy and was at last able to accept forgiveness.

Mercy

When we are captives of our guilt, God's grace comes to us in the form of mercy. To speak of God's mercy is not to speak of a sentimental attitude that does not care about the abuses of yesterday. To be merciful is to do something more profound than to overlook wrong that has been done. To be merciful is to do something more than simply not care how rotten a person was in the past. Nor is it to play a game of pretending the past wrongs never happened.

Mercy cares. Mercy is concerned about the wrong that was done, but it cares *more* about the potential for good that remains. This concern for the positive potential that remains is what makes the restoration of relationships at least a possibility. Out of an awareness of the good that yet can be, mercy offers the possibility of a new relationship.

The motivation to be merciful does not come from focusing on the past. It comes from focusing on the present and future possibilities. I have never been able to be merciful when I was focusing on the wrong someone did to me yesterday. It is only when I am able to sense the remaining positive possibilities in that relationship that I am able to be merciful.

The motivation for mercy is clearly related to an awareness of the positive potential that is present. The mother is merciful toward each of her children because she is aware of the positive potential in each child. To say

God is merciful is to say God is more concerned about the good that is yet possible than about all of the bad that has already been done. The past is past and cannot be undone. What remain are the present and the future. God's mercy is driven by the longing for the present and future to be released from bondage to past sin and set loose to fulfill the potential God sees.

This is true even though the good that seems possible appears to be small in comparison with the wrong that has been done. God does not view life the way we do. Jesus said to the thief on the cross, "Today you will be with me in Paradise" (Luke 23:43). Christ cared more about fulfilling the potential for good in that moment than he did about all the past wrongs the thief had done. To be sure, the thief did not escape the consequences of his yesterdays (nor do we). He was still a thief being executed on a cross. But in that situation, with all of its severe limitations, God through Christ was concerned for the thief to fulfill his remaining potential. God in Christ was more concerned about the relationship that could yet be with that penitent thief than with the crimes in his past.

To say God is merciful is to acknowledge that God is more concerned about fulfilling the potential left in us than he is with "getting even" for all our past failures. God's focus is not on the past. God's focus is on the possibilities of fulfilling the best that is within us—even if now we are like that thief dying on his cross. Even in that kind of situation God focuses on our potential. What makes grace in the form of mercy so amazing is that regardless of our past we continue to be important to God.

In our grief we need the grace of God's mercy. It is very easy for us to become locked in the prison of remembering our failures. It is very easy for us to allow our abuses of the past to fill us with feelings of guilt, and when we are tangled in the web of guilt, we miss the possibilities present today. We need to receive God's mercy that focuses on the present, positive potential. We need to receive this mercy from God so that we can be merciful to ourselves and others, focusing on what God sees in them and us—positive potential.

How Grace Comes

How does this aspect of God's grace come to us? The primary instrument God uses to give us grace is other people. Grace comes through what they do; sometimes it comes through what they refuse to do—the burdens they refuse to put on our backs. It comes through their compassion and love; it comes through their knowledge and the insights they share. God uses people who are near us and people who live far away. God uses people we love and people we hardly know. His grace comes through words people have written long ago. It even comes through the memory of persons we have not seen for years.

Sometimes it is the memory of other persons and their faith that keeps us going. I quoted a verse from Psalm 51 above. Some say this psalm is a poem David wrote after his affair with Bathsheba and his ordering her husband to be killed in battle. Whoever wrote it was caught in the agony of guilt. One of the ways grace came to him was in the memory of a promise: "a broken and contrite heart, O

God, thou wilt not despise" (Psalm 51:17). Even though he did not yet feel the release of forgiveness, he found strength to endure by remembering the promise of forgiveness.

One of the ways God's grace comes to us in the midst of our guilt feelings is in our remembering the promises of the gospel that have been handed down to us. Here again God has used people to make his grace known—the people who have taught us about the promises in the gospel.

Jesus said, "For where two or three are gathered in my name, there am I in the midst of them" (Matthew 18:20). He said this while he was talking to the disciples about forgiveness. Whatever else this passage may mean, it clearly implies that Christ—the grace of God—comes to us through community in our interaction with one another.

But it is not every community through which grace flows. It is the community of two or more "gathered in my name." To be gathered in the name of Christ is something more profound than meeting together under a Christian label. As most of us know, some groups of people who call themselves Christians have said and done cruel, mean things.

For the Jews of Bible times the word *name* referred to more than a label. For them it referred to the essence, the basic quality, the identifying reality. When the Bible speaks of a group who are gathered "in the name of Christ," it is talking about a group that has as its basic quality or characteristic, the basic quality and characteristics that identified Christ, namely, the love of God.

We are most likely to receive grace, especially grace in the form of forgiveness or mercy, in a group characterized by the love of God. This group may or may not talk a lot about Jesus, but it will definitely be a group in which there is the kind of love made known in Jesus the Christ. It will be a group "gathered in my name."

Sometimes this group is found within a congregation, sometimes among peers at work, sometimes among friends in the neighborhood. Sometimes the group is just you and one other person. Sometimes the group is composed of many members.

Sometimes the grace of God comes through the people we expected it to come through; sometimes we are quite surprised by the persons God uses to deliver his grace. Because we can never say in advance whom God is going to use to deliver grace, we dare not shut ourselves off from people—the primary instruments God uses to deliver us from our distress.

One more practical word needs to be stated. Sometimes we have special needs. Sometimes our feelings of guilt continue to plague us for a long period of time. When this happens, it may be a signal that we need to seek trained help. In almost every community there is at least one pastor who has developed special counseling skills. Most pastors know psychologists or psychiatrists who can help. The availability of these persons is another expression of God's grace. They are among the instruments God uses in distributing his merciful, life transforming grace.

8 *Dealing with Fears and Doubts*

Insecurity

The feeling of insecurity is sometimes part of the grief process. A person who has been important to us is dead; a significant relationship we relied on has ended. Not only do we feel lonely and become more aware of our basic aloneness (see chapter 4 above), we also experience some form of fear. What we had in the past, we will not have in the future. Ways of living that were familiar and comfortable have been disrupted, and we realize it will never be the same again. This awareness of "the way things really are" can create in us a sense of insecurity, if not outright fear.

"I am afraid," June said. "It is a strange kind of fear. It is like being on top of a tall building and looking over the edge and realizing there is no guardrail. I know I am safe on the roof, and yet there is no guardrail to keep me from falling over the edge. Daddy had been my guardrail. I did not lean on him, but just knowing he was there if I needed him made me feel secure. Now that he is gone, I feel this strange kind of fear. I feel vulnerable, as if there is no one to protect me from falling over the edge."

Anxiety

Frequently the kind of fear grief causes is anxiety. When we are anxious, we are afraid, but we do not know exactly what we fear. Engulfed by our grief, we look into our future and feel insecure. We begin to realize we are going to have to live without someone who has been very important to us, and we doubt being able to fill the gap caused by this death. We doubt our ability to deal with all that lies ahead and experience anxiety.

Marie was an elderly woman who had never taken care of business matters. When her husband died, not only did she feel lonely, she was also anxious. Her outlook on what remained of her life filled her with dread and fear. The one who had taken care of her was dead, and now everything was her responsibility.

Marie doubted she could do it. She was afraid she would make a fool of herself. She was afraid she would be made fun of for not knowing how to take care of her money. She was afraid someone would take advantage of her ignorance and cheat her out of what little she had. She was afraid of having to experience the humiliation of poverty. She was afraid of becoming just a Social Security number in an impersonal, public nursing home. She was afraid she would die neglected and alone. When she looked into the future, all these fears welded together into one big nameless fear. Doubting her ability to cope with all this, she experienced painful anxiety.

Bill's anxieties, fears, and doubts were different from Marie's. His wife died when she was only twenty-six, leaving him with their four-year-old daughter, Ella. He worried about being able to provide the kind of guidance and affection their daughter needed. He doubted that he would have enough emotional energy for the combined demands of his job and the personal needs of his daughter. He did not have a specific fear as much as he experienced great anxiety regarding his future and the future Ella.

Fear of a Different Future

Without the person who meant so much to us, the future can seem frightening. In grief we can be so overwhelmed by what we have lost, we feel terribly—even hopelessly—inadequate. What lies ahead is a life that appears to be very new and strange. Aware of our loss and the very different kind of living that is ahead, we doubt our abilities.

Fear of the future and doubts about our abilities are not the only expressions of fear and doubt that are sometimes part of our grief. The death of someone who is close to us can wake our anxieties and fears regarding death itself.

Fear of Death

"I had never really thought much about death until Dad died. Then it dawned on me, really dawned on me, that death is real. I guess that sounds silly. Of course, I knew in my head I would die someday; but when Dad died, something happened inside me. I think for the first time in my life I was really aware that I too will die. It really scared me. I began feeling that I had only a little time left. I began suspecting every little ache was a sign of some fatal illness. I could not talk about any of this then. I guess I was both afraid and ashamed of my fear. Anyway, I did not say anything to anyone."

"What happened to Granddaddy?" the little girl asked.

"He died; he got so sick he could not get well," her mother answered.

"But what happened to him when he died?"

The little girl's question is our question when we face death. It is a factor in our fears. What happens? Death is an unknown. Unknowns can be frightening.

I remember a conversation I had when I was going to college. Several of us were discussing what we thought happened or did not happen after death. We talked about whether or not there is some sort of life after death. We rambled on about persons who were never "Christian," and yet who seemed to love God and neighbor. What happened to them when they died? Is there really a heaven and a hell? What about the "bad people" who did not know any better? It was a typical sophomore's religious "bull session." There was probably more noise than substance to it. Certainly more issues were raised than were settled.

Dr. Ennis Hill, who was then pastor of the First Methodist Church in San Angelo, Texas, quietly listened to our discussion. Finally someone asked him what he thought. He said, "Do you believe God is the wisest of the wise, and that God really is a God of love?"

"Well, yes," we replied.

"Then," Dr. Hill smiled, "Why worry? Whatever is wisest and most loving is what will happen in death. We may not be able to say exactly what that is, but because God is wise and loving, we do not have to worry about it."

The Common Sense of Faith

Dr. Hill's response is what I call the common sense of faith. It takes faith to be able to believe what he said. But, having faith, his statement is only common sense. Dr. Hill's profoundly simple response said in effect: "You say God can be trusted; well, trust God."

In dealing with the fears and doubts that come in our grief (such as those described in this chapter), the *basic* issue has to do with trusting God. Can we trust God to provide what we need in our new situation? Can we trust God to help us face our drastically altered lives? Can we trust God as we face our own deaths? Can God be trusted?

When we ask this question (whatever the form) we are not asking a question with our heads as much as we are asking a question with our hearts. Aching with grief and tangled in feelings of fears and doubt, we do not want academic, theological proof that God can be trusted. We yearn for a more personal assurance that speaks to our hearts. On another day, when the experiences of grief are less intense, we will be ready for a more orderly and disciplined dealing with the theological issues that are involved. In our anguish we long for assurances more than for arguments; we long for witnesses more than for lectures.

Perhaps the reason we are impatient with persons who want to give us theology lessons in the midst of our grief is we are intuitively aware that what we need is faith, and faith does not come at the end of an argument. How faith comes to us is a mystery. We seek it, and yet it always comes as a gift of grace.

Some Ways Grace Comes

God's grace comes in many ways. For example, one of the ways in which God supplied courage to Ruth (the woman whose husband had always taken care of her) was in her memory of what Aunt Louise had gone through.

Ruth remembered that Aunt Louise was twenty-eight when her husband died in 1904. She was left with three sons, ages three, five, and eight. In those horse-and-buggy days, she lived on a ranch that was ten miles from the nearest town, two miles from the nearest neighbor, and hundreds of miles from the nearest relative. Before she married, Louise had never lived on a ranch. There were none of the conveniences we take for granted, such as a telephone that could be used to call for help, or a car to drive quickly into town for supplies, or running water that made cooking and cleaning easier. Louise stayed on the ranch and somehow she survived until she learned enough about ranching to do more than merely survive. Although most people had said she would fail, she did not. Her sons matured to became respected men in the area, and her ranch made more than a comfortable living. It grew in size so that it could be divided into three ranches; one for each of her sons. Ruth remembered Aunt Louise, and she drew courage from her memories.

In our grief, each of us can draw on our memories. We can remember other persons who have gone through ordeals similar to ours. We remember they made it with the help of God, and we can trust we will make it also. We can remember difficult times we have survived in the past. God was helping us then (whether we realized it or not), and God will not forget us now.

Another way that God's grace can come to us is through our awareness of the wisdom to be found in our Judeo-Christian heritage, especially in some of the Bible stories.

For example, one of the classic stories having to do with whether or not God can be trusted is the story about the promise God made to Abraham. Part of God's promise (Genesis 12:1–3) was that Abraham would be the father of a multitude, a great nation. But year after year Abraham and Sarah were childless. Throughout the decades of childlessness, God kept reminding Abraham of the promise. Could God be trusted? Genesis chapter 17 tells about Abraham as a very old man laughing when once again God declared the promise. The story in chapter 18 has Sarah laughing at God's promise. But the baby came. God kept his promise.

God did not forget his people in Egyptian slavery; God kept his promise. God did not abandon his people when they were in Babylon; he kept his promise. God did not allow the crucifixion of Jesus to remain a defeat; God transformed it into victory through the resurrection; God kept his promise. Over and over the stories of the Bible remind us that God can be trusted. Our awareness of the wisdom in these stories can be one of the ways God's grace comes to us when we are tangled in the doubts and fears of grief.

One of the verses of the popular hymn "Amazing Grace" has been especially meaningful to me, not only in times of grief, but also in other difficult times:

> Through many dangers, toils and snares,
>
> > I have already come;
>
> 'tis grace hath brought me safe thus far,
>
> > and grace will lead me home.[1]

As stated earlier, people are the primary instruments God uses to give us the grace we need. God uses persons such as Aunt Louise and Abraham and Sarah. He uses the people who have kept the stories of Aunt Louise and Abraham alive for us. God also uses the neighbor who lives next door or the person who works with us or with whom we go fishing. It is persons such as these whom God uses to meet our mundane and practical needs. The man who had never operated a washing machine until his wife died was helped by his next-door neighbor. Marie's fear that she could not take care of business matters is the kind of fear that God can heal through a neighbor's help and concern.

One of the ways we humans block this expression of God's grace is by our unwillingness to ask for help. While we may be willing to ask God in secret for help, we are unwilling to admit our need to a neighbor. Although our unwillingness to ask a friend to help is frequently rationalized as, "I don't want to be a bother," more often than not our refusing to ask for help is a symptom of our pride and a rejection of humility.

1. John Newton (1725–1807), "Amazing Grace."

What else is humility but the open admission of need? Our unwillingness to admit our need to friends makes our prayers to God hollow. We are saying: "God help me but do not allow anyone to see that I need anything." It is as if we asked God to help and then tied his hands.

Our pride can block God's grace. The grace is there; it is given. All we have to do is ask and receive it. Jesus talked about the importance of asking (see Luke 11:5–13). Just as the Pharisees blocked their ability to receive the available forgiveness by refusing to admit their sin, we block our ability to receive the grace offered us in our grief by refusing to admit our needs.

Summary

Fears and doubts are often part of our grief. But God makes grace available to us. It comes to us in a variety of ways. In this chapter we have looked at only three of those ways. It comes through our memories of other persons; it comes through our awareness of the wisdom in the Judeo-Christian heritage, and it comes through the practical help we can receive from other people. In a variety of ways God's grace is at work among us to give us courage, strength, confidence and hope in the midst of our grief.

Jesus said, "Ask, and it will be given you" (Luke 11:9).

9 *Hiding Our Grief*

Some Reasons Why We Hide Our Grief

"How are you getting along?" It was clear from the tone of the question that Mark was not merely making polite conversation.

"Oh, I'm doing okay," Jack replied, not really stating the truth. He knew Mark was genuinely concerned, but Jack was reluctant, even afraid, to share his deep ache and sadness. Only three weeks had passed since the funeral of his daughter. Jack was afraid he would cry if he allowed himself to start talking about his grief and intense sorrow. That might cause Mark to feel uncomfortable, and he thought that would be embarrassing and awkward for both men.

Mark had opened the door to allow Jack to share his grief, but Jack was afraid to go through it. He hid his grief rather than risk crying in front of his friend. It was not just pride at work. It was also Jack's concern for Mark. Jack hid the depth of his sorrow because he did not want to cause his friend to be made to feel uncomfortable.

The further we move from the time of the death, the more difficult it is for many of us to admit or express the sorrow in our grief. There seems to be an unwritten law in many parts of our society that says it is okay to cry at the time of death and at the time of the funeral but not weeks later. It is as though there is a social expectation that we should get all our emotionally intense sorrow over with in a few days and then move on. When tears come later, all too often we who shed the tears and those who are near us feel shades of awkwardness and embarrassment when sorrow breaks loose in tears.

So, after the first few crisis days of the death and funeral, we tend to keep our grief inside ourselves. We do not want to impose on our friends or cause them to feel uncomfortable. We do not want to risk exposing our friends' inability to cope with our grief. We choose to grieve alone rather than risk causing a friend to feel awkward or inadequate. So we keep our grief to ourselves. This is especially true for men but not only for men.

"After all," we tell ourselves, "what could they do, anyway?"

This temptation to hide our grief after the first few days is somewhat encouraged by attitudes toward death in our society. Many people in our culture find it difficult to deal with the reality of death, and this hampers their ability to deal with the grief of others. So in our not wanting to burden others, we attempt to hide our grief, especially our sorrow.

But once we begin to hide our grief from others, it is not long until we are trying to hide our grief from ourselves.

We are a "fix-it" culture that likes to do things quickly. We want fast, practical results. We are aware our friends want to *do* something "to make it better," yet there is very little they can *do*. Afraid that their inability to "fix it" will cause our friends to feel inadequate and awkward, we hide our grief. After my father's death my fear of causing friends to feel awkward in the presence of my grief motivated me to try to keep my grief to myself. I tried to hide it from them, and in the process I discovered the easiest way to do that was to also hide it from myself.

A Congenial Conspiracy

In our grief, we often find ourselves caught in a cycle of behavior that is not helpful. We do not want our friends to feel inadequate; therefore, we do not talk about anything that might trigger our sorrow. Our friends pick up signals from us that "we would rather not talk about it." So they try to help us by not talking about anything they fear might cause us to feel sad.

In their attempt to help us, it is not unusual for our friends to give the dead person the silent treatment whenever we are near. It is as if our friends had never known the person who died. Yet how helpful it would be for us to talk and cry and laugh together as we share our memories! But our friends are afraid of upsetting us, and we are afraid of causing them to feel awkward. Thus we join in a congenial conspiracy to deny our grief.

This unexpressed agreement to avoid stimulating or exposing our grief creates the illusion that our grief is ending only a short time after it began. In truth, the grief has merely gone underground.

In this period of publicly silent grief, some of us begin to think, "There must be something wrong with me; the funeral was weeks ago, and yet I am still grieving." This is especially true when we do not experience our most intense sorrow until months after the funeral (see chapter 2).

No Timetable

Grief has no timetable, anymore than grief has a set pattern for all people. Each grief experience is unique. One of the dangers in a little book like this is of creating the illusion the process of grief is a fixed process. It is not. The grief each person experiences is a unique happening. This is certainly true regarding the length of time each person experiences the more intense feelings of grief, especially sorrow.

These intense feelings come and go like storm waves washing over a beach; the waves are high and forceful. For some the storm begins immediately; for others the most intense feelings of sorrow come much later. When the intense sorrow comes, it does not come once and then is gone. It comes and goes. There are periods of relative calm, but they are like the calm in the eye of a hurricane. The storm is not over. For some persons the waves come and go for only a few days. For others this period of fairly frequent experiences of intense sorrow lasts several weeks, sometimes even several months. When our grief is related to the death of someone with whom we had a very close relationship, even years later there can be moments when a wave of intense sorrow washes over us.

The length of time it takes to work through these waves of intense feelings is not important. What is important is that we work through them. What is important is that we not allow the uncomfortable feelings others may have in the presence of our sorrow to lure us to deny or hide our grief.

Grief Like a River

To try to deny our grief is like trying to stop a river from flowing. We may succeed in building a dam and not allowing any water downstream, but the water backs up and floods other ground. We may dam our grief's more natural expressions; however, the steady flow of its reality will cause it to flood into other areas of our living. Building a dam (denying our grief) does not stop the water from flowing; it merely blocks the water from its natural course and causes it to seek other outlets.

Bill tried to cut his grief, especially his sorrow, short. His emotions found other outlets. He became quick tempered. The slightest aggravation caused him to explode. He was hypercritical of everyone who worked with him. He blocked his sorrow by denying his grief but his temper overflowed.

Sue swallowed her grief. It did not overflow in outward anger. Her denied grief welled up inside her and was experienced as significant depression.

Grief Is Part of Life

Grief is not something we need to hide as if it were something to be ashamed of. Grief is part of life. The Bible reminds us that part of what it is to be fully human is to grieve and experience sorrow. The writer of Ecclesiastes declares that in life there is not only a time to dance, there is also a time to mourn (3:4). Jesus experienced sorrow to the point of weeping (John 11:35). Grief, especially in the form of sorrow, stands at the crossroads of love and mortality.

We humans can love; we humans are mortal; therefore, grief is inevitable. Grief happens when love has to deal with the limitations placed on life, especially the limitation of death. The only way we could avoid grief and sorrow is to avoid caring and loving. But that is no choice at all. Our grief is the inevitable consequence of being mortal creatures who love.

An Opportunity

Yet we can say more than that grief is an inevitable experience in life. We can find the motivation we need to face our grief when we realize grief can be an opportunity for growth. It is certainly *not* the kind of opportunity we choose. Grief is a painful experience that is thrust upon us. But once we find ourselves in the anguish of grief, we can use this experience for growth. In fact, we either use the experience of grief for growth, or we suffer some sort of decay.

Who can say what types of growth a person can experience in the midst of grief? Through their struggles with grief, some people might discover new talents and opportunities. My mother did as she worked through her grieving the death of my father. They had married when she was eighteen, and at age fifty-eight she discovered abilities she had not needed to develop until then. Some people might grow in their ability to accept love. Others might discover new depths in their lives and in their faith. Others might reevaluate their priorities. Others may discover or rediscover in a more profound way, the importance of friends. Still others may discover a more profound faith. Who can say what others might discover?

It is not important to list all the ways grief can stimulate growth. It is important to be aware that grief (never desired and always painful) can be used for good. We do not have to look on it as a burden to be hidden or denied. It is a burden, to be sure, but it can be a burden that has positive potential within it—a positive potential that can be realized only by facing the grief and working through it.

All this is to say God's grace can and does work through our grief. Therefore it is neither appropriate nor helpful to us to try to deny or repress our grief. Our denials are only roadblocks in the way of God's grace.

Dealing with the Discomfort of Our Friends

But what about the uncomfortable feelings our friends seem to have? What shall we do?

We shall love our friends enough to allow them to love us. An amazing thing about love is that when it is expressed in a mature way, it is a two-way reality; it helps the ones we love, and we also receive some benefits. When our love for our friends is mature, we are honest with them. The more mature we are, the more we are willing to give our friends the chance to be our friends by letting them know that we need them. Is there any bigger gift than the gift of being needed?

In our grief we need other people. To be sure, there is a dimension of our grief that only we can know, and that only we can endure in solitude. But a primary source of strength, one of the primary ways we are strengthened by God's grace, is through the love we receive from others.

How helpful it would have been to both Mark and Jack if Jack could have reached out to Mark.

"How are you getting along?" It was clear from the tone of the question that Mark was not just making polite conversation.

"Oh, in terms of the surface routines, I guess I'm okay. But, Mark, the ache is still there." (Tears come to his eyes.) "There are times when I don't think I can make it."

"It must be rough. Is there *anything* I can do to help?" It is obvious that Mark is somewhat uneasy, but it is also obvious that Mark really cares.

"Just having friends like you helps. It really does."

No problems were solved. There were no great break-throughs into new, profound insights. It was simply an experience of intimacy, but it is through such experiences that we receive the grace we need to cope with our grief.

Anyone who has shared in such a simple and intimate experience is aware of the mystery that strengthens bonds of friendship. Jack loved Mark enough to share his grief. In the sharing of his grief he found new depth and strength in his friendship with Mark.

This can happen to us only if we refuse to hide our grief. When we do not "play games" with our grief, then, one of the ways God's grace can come to us is through our friends' love.

10   *Moving beyond Grief to New Life*

God provides what we need from the moment we enter grief until slowly, gradually we discover we have made it through the dark valley without being destroyed.

What is on the other side of grief? Beyond grief we discover new life. Just as each experience of grief is unique, the new life each of us discovers is different.

Two Illustrations

Mrs. Roberts loved her husband. They had been married more than forty years when he died. Opportunities open to women today were not a realistic option when they married. During their many years of marriage, they developed a comfortable and creative relationship. She found meaning and contentment in helping her husband with his work. Both he and she understood his vocation to be "their" work. She depended on him, and he depended on her. They were a team, a unit, and much of her sense of satisfaction and accomplishment came from her contributing to their (not just his) success.

When Mr. Roberts died, she felt as if the world had collapsed. Her grief was painful and long. She had never lived alone. The doubts and fears that come with grief made her tremble. But she moved on. She moved into a new life.

She faced each day. She lived one day at a time until she had enough confidence to begin to face the future. She began to do the work her husband had done and became involved in activities she would not have had the time or the desire to do if Mr. Roberts was alive. She was so effective in her labors she received some recognition. Her friends saw her in a new light, and she began to have a new view of herself.

To this day, Mrs. Roberts wishes her husband was alive, growing old with her. But that was not an option. The only choice Mrs. Roberts had was to move on to a new life or to decay by trying to hang on to yesterday. Mrs. Roberts chose life.

She has worked through the grief process. This is not to say that she is no longer touched by moments of sadness. One time she was visiting her son. He took her through the place where he worked, showing her what he had accomplished. She was proud. She longed for Mr. Roberts to be there to share this moment with her. Tears came to her eyes.

When we have loved deeply, that love stays with us. Because it is *love,* from time to time we are painfully aware of what we have lost.

Linda was only ten years old when she died. In her long illness she developed a wisdom and faith many children who know they are facing death attain. Her parents,

Ron and Julie, could not believe she was dead. For years they had fought her disease. They had been told what to expect, but when it finally happened, they were not ready. They could not imagine life without Linda.

Their grief was lengthy, their anguish extreme. They had an especially difficult struggle with their anger. "Why would God allow this to happen?" Bitterness and resentment threatened to take over their lives.

Finally they began to emerge from their grief. Ron and Julie continue to miss Linda. Even now that they are through the grief process, there are moments of intense sorrow. Although they have conquered the temptation to become bitter, they do not like what happened. They wish she was alive and healthy. But they have faced reality. She is dead. Their choice has been the same as Mrs. Roberts's. They could face a new life without Linda, or they could dwell on the past and decay. They chose life.

Ron said the turning point for him came one day while he was in the midst of mentally ranting: "Why did she have to die? Why did this happen to her? Why did this happen to us?" Then he was stopped short by a different question that came into his mind and heart: "Why should we have ever had Linda for our daughter? Why are we the ones who have been blessed by her short life?"

As these questions became more and more unavoidable, their grieving took on a different flavor. It was not that their grief disappeared, but this new set of questions added the reality of gratitude into their grief.

From their ordeal they gained a new view of life. They saw how precious and fragile life is. They saw how big a gift life is. They discovered the basic question is not, why is there tragedy? The basic question is, why is life so good that tragedy is a possibility? In the pain of their grief over what they had lost, they were able to celebrate the gifts they had been given.

I have known others who were saved from bondage to bitterness and resentment by discovering the gift of gratitude in the midst of grief. The gift of being grateful is truly a gift of grace, especially in the midst of grief.

The Purpose of This Little Book

The purpose of this book has been to describe the complexity of grief and to point to some of the ways God's grace is at work in our grief. When we accept the gifts of grace, we are able to affirm life and our lives, even when life and our lives are not the way we want.

In "Introducing Grace and Grief" above we looked at verse 4 of the Psalm 23:

> Even though I walk through the valley of the shadow
> of death,
> I will fear no evil;
> for thou art with me;
> thy rod and thy staff,
> they comfort me.

Throughout this book I have tried to describe some ways that God's grace is with us in our grief, pushing and pulling us through. Because of this grace, we have the strength to face life and the power to move on.

There is another verse from this psalm that is also appropriate for us to remember as we go through grief.

> Thou preparest a table before me
>> in the presence of my enemies;
> Thou anointest my head with oil,
>> my cup overflows. (Psalm 23:5)

Life has a way of sitting us down in the presence of that which could destroy us—our enemies. We do not choose grief, and yet grief comes. Grief sits at our table of life like an enemy that would destroy us. It is helpful to remember the poet of Psalm 23 was aware that the table is a prepared table. It is a place where he could be nourished.

God nourishes us, even in the presence of the very enemies that would destroy us. Circumstances in life from time to time place us in a situation we do not choose, and it is a dangerous situation. But, we need not be destroyed; even there God provides resources to give us strength to face what must be faced and the power to move on. Even when life sits us down in the presence of what could destroy us, the nourishment that comes through the ways God's amazing grace is at work in our lives is there also.

Not only can we be nourished, we can be blessed: "You anoint my head with oil, my cup overflows." We are given more than we need to survive. We are given more than life; we are given life with an eternal quality, an abundant life.

Mrs. Roberts, Ron, and Julie did not choose their grief. But, as painful as their grief was, they were not destroyed. They were nourished, even in their grief. They discovered life beyond grief, not life as it had been but a new life—a gift of God's grace.

For Further Reading

For Everyone:

Brueggemann, Walter. *Praying the Psalms: Engaging Scripture and the Life of the Spirit.* 2nd ed. Eugene, OR: Cascade Books, 2007.

Goldberg, Michael. *Raising Spirits: Stories of Suffering and Comfort at Death's Door.* Eugene, OR: Cascade Books, 2010.

Mayer, Donald E. *Letters to Peter: On the Journey from Grief to Wholeness.* Eugene, OR: Cascade Books, 2010.

Strommen, Merton P., and A. Irene Strommen. *Five Cries of Grief: One Family's Journey to Healing after the Tragic Death of a Son.* San Francisco: HarperSanFranciso, 1993.

Wolterstorff, Nicholas. *Lament for a Son.* Grand Rapids: Eerdmans, 1987.

For Pastors:

Kelley, Melissa M. *Grief: Contemporary Theory and the Practice of Ministry.* Minneapolis: Fortress, 2010.

Oates, Wayne E. *Grief, Transition, and Loss: A Pastor's Practical Guide.* Creative Pastoral Care and Counseling Series. Minneapolis: Fortress, 1997.

Rambo, Shelly. *Spirit and Trauma: A Theology of Remaining.* Louisville: Westminster John Knox, 2010.

Tournier, Paul. *Guilt and Grace: A Psychological Study.* Translated by Arthur W. Heathcote et al. New York: Harper, 1962.

Zurheide, Jeffry R. *When Faith Is Tested: Pastoral Responses to Suffering and Tragic Death.* Creative Pastoral Care and Counseling Series. Minneapolis: Fortress, 1997.